GENESIS EXPLAINED

GENESIS EXPLAINED

Understanding the Book and Its Message for Today

Samuel Whitaker

Part of the Bible for Modern Life Series

Ascent Press

Published by
Ascent Press

ISBN: 979-8-9997184-6-4

Printed in the United States of America

First Edition 2026

For those seeking clarity in the ancient words of Scripture.

CONTENTS

Disclaimer

This book provides an interpretive overview of the biblical text using historical scholarship and modern analysis tools. It is intended to help readers understand the themes, context, and message of the biblical narrative and is not intended to replace personal study of Scripture.

About the Bible for Modern Life Series

Each book in this series explores one book of the Bible through historical context, narrative explanation, and modern reflection. The goal is to help readers understand what the text says, what it meant in its original setting, and how its themes still speak to modern life.

Why Read the Bible Again?

Across thousands of years, the Bible has remained one of the most influential collections of writings in human history. Entire civilizations have been shaped by its stories, its moral vision, and its portrayal of humanity's relationship with God. Its language has shaped literature, law, art, and culture across continents. Yet despite this influence, many modern readers approach the Bible with uncertainty.

Some see it as an ancient religious text that belongs to a distant world. Others remember fragments of stories heard in childhood but struggle to understand how those stories connect to modern life. Many people are curious about the Bible but feel intimidated by its length, its unfamiliar cultural setting, or the centuries of debate surrounding its interpretation.

At the same time, the questions that run through the Bible remain deeply familiar.

Why does the world contain both beauty and suffering? Why do individuals struggle with pride, fear, jealousy, and ambition?

Why do families experience conflict across generations?

How can people live with integrity in a complicated world?

Is redemption possible when mistakes and failures accumulate?

These questions are not new. They have existed as long as human history itself. What makes the Bible remarkable is that it confronts these questions directly through narrative, poetry, reflection, and historical memory.

The purpose of this series is to help modern readers approach the Bible with clarity and confidence.

Rather than assuming specialized theological training or deep familiarity with ancient history, each book in this series walks carefully through one book of the Bible at a time. The goal is not simply to summarize the text, but to help readers understand what the book says, what it meant within its original cultural setting, and how its themes continue to speak into modern experience.

Each volume follows a consistent structure designed to make the text accessible.

First, the book begins by identifying the core human question that the biblical text addresses. Every book of the Bible speaks to a fundamental human struggle. Genesis explores the origins of the world and the problem of human brokenness. Job wrestles with the mystery of suffering. Ecclesiastes examines the search for meaning in a world that often feels unpredictable. The New Testament letters consider how transformation and faith can shape daily life.

Understanding these questions provides a starting point for reading the text.

Next, each volume offers orientation. Readers are introduced to the historical setting of the book, its traditional authorship, and its place within the larger biblical story. The Bible is not a single book written at one moment in history. It is a library of writings produced across centuries and cultures. Recognizing where each book fits helps readers understand how the narrative develops over time.

After orientation, the series explores the world behind the book. Ancient geography, political structures, cultural practices, and religious traditions all shape how biblical stories unfold.

Understanding this environment helps modern readers see why certain events occur and why particular themes appear repeatedly.

The central portion of each volume then walks through the narrative or argument of the book itself. Narrative texts are explained through the unfolding story. Letters and teachings are examined through their central ideas. Wisdom literature is explored through the themes that connect its reflections.

The goal is clarity.

Rather than overwhelming readers with technical debates, the focus remains on understanding the flow of the text and the ideas it communicates.

Once the structure of the book becomes clear, several key themes are identified. These themes often echo across the entire Bible: creation and responsibility, covenant and faithfulness, justice and mercy, human failure and the possibility of restoration. Recognizing these patterns helps readers see how individual stories contribute to a larger narrative.

Another important section addresses common misunderstandings. Over time, certain passages have been interpreted in ways that obscure the original message of the text. Sometimes modern readers impose contemporary assumptions onto ancient writings. Other times, popular debates focus attention on issues that the original audience would not have considered central. Clarifying these misunderstandings allows the text to speak more clearly.

From there, the series turns toward modern life. The world described in the Bible is culturally distant from modern society, yet the underlying human experiences remain strikingly familiar. Leadership challenges, family conflict, ethical dilemmas, ambition, fear, forgiveness, and hope appear in every generation. The themes explored in each biblical book are therefore translated into situations that readers recognize today.

This connection between ancient narrative and modern experience is essential.

The Bible was never intended to function only as a historical artifact. Its stories and reflections were preserved because communities believed they contained wisdom for life.

Finally, each volume concludes with reflection questions and practical lessons drawn from the themes of the book. These sections invite readers to consider how the ideas explored throughout the text might shape their own decisions, relationships, and sense of purpose.

The aim is not to provide rigid formulas or simple answers.

Instead, the goal is thoughtful engagement.

The Bible contains both profound insight and complex questions. It presents moments of extraordinary faith alongside stories of human failure. It describes hope in the middle of suffering and redemption in situations that appear beyond repair.

For many readers, approaching the Bible for the first time—or returning to it after many years—can feel like stepping into unfamiliar territory. This series is designed to make that journey easier. By moving through the text one book at a time, readers can gradually see how the larger narrative unfolds.

The journey begins with Genesis.

Genesis explores the origins of the world, the emergence of human freedom and responsibility, and the beginnings of a promise that shapes the rest of the biblical story. It asks one of the most enduring questions in human history:

Why is the world broken?

And it begins to offer an answer that will continue to unfold across the pages of Scripture.

Introduction

Why Genesis Still Matters

Genesis stands at the beginning of the Bible, but its influence reaches far beyond its opening pages. The stories contained in this ancient text have shaped cultures, informed moral traditions, and influenced the imagination of countless generations. Even people who have never read Genesis often recognize its most famous scenes: the creation of the world, the Garden of Eden, the flood of Noah, the tower of Babel, and the journeys of Abraham and his descendants.

Yet Genesis is more than a collection of familiar stories. It forms the foundation for the entire biblical narrative. Without Genesis, the rest of the Bible loses much of its context, because themes that appear later in Scripture—covenant, redemption, faith, and restoration—are introduced here and developed throughout the rest of the biblical story.

The book asks a set of questions that remain deeply relevant today. Why does the world contain both beauty and brokenness? Why do human beings possess such extraordinary creativity while also displaying a capacity for conflict and destruction? Why do families experience both love and division? Why do individuals struggle with trust, ambition, fear, and responsibility?

Genesis approaches these questions through narrative rather than abstract philosophy. Instead of presenting arguments about human nature, the book tells stories. Through these stories, readers encounter individuals whose lives reflect the complexity of the human condition. These characters are not distant or idealized figures. They are deeply recognizable people navigating difficult decisions and uncertain circumstances.

Abraham leaves his homeland without knowing where his journey will lead. Jacob spends years wrestling with the consequences of deception and family conflict. Joseph faces betrayal, slavery, and imprisonment before discovering a purpose hidden within his suffering. Their stories unfold across deserts, cities, and unfamiliar landscapes, yet the emotional terrain they navigate remains familiar to modern readers, where fear influences decisions, ambition creates tension, trust becomes fragile, and forgiveness proves difficult but necessary.

The power of Genesis lies in its ability to portray these realities honestly while still pointing toward hope. The book begins with the creation of a world described as orderly and good, where humanity is placed with both freedom and responsibility. Yet the narrative quickly reveals how easily that freedom can be misused. A single act of disobedience introduces consequences that shape the rest of the human story, as relationships fracture, work becomes difficult, trust erodes, and the world begins to reflect both dignity and brokenness.

Genesis does not avoid these tensions. Instead, it traces how they develop across generations. The first family experiences jealousy and violence. Communities become defined by corruption and pride. Human ambition attempts to secure identity through power and achievement. Yet the narrative never settles into despair. Again and again, moments of failure are followed by unexpected grace. Noah survives a flood that reshapes the world. Abraham receives a promise that his family will become a blessing to future nations. Joseph rises from imprisonment to leadership, eventually saving the very brothers who betrayed him.

These stories reveal a recurring pattern. Human weakness appears repeatedly, yet the possibility of restoration continues to emerge. Genesis therefore functions as both an explanation and a beginning. It explains how the world came to contain both beauty and conflict, purpose and uncertainty, while also introducing a promise that begins to move the story toward redemption.

The events described in Genesis unfold within a cultural setting very different from the modern world. The societies portrayed in the text rely on agriculture, travel along caravan routes, and organize themselves through extended families and tribal relationships. Political authority is often localized rather than centralized in large empires. Understanding this ancient setting helps readers interpret the narrative more clearly, yet it also becomes apparent that the deeper human struggles described in Genesis remain strikingly familiar.

Modern societies possess technologies that ancient cultures could never have imagined. Cities are larger, communication is faster, and scientific knowledge has expanded dramatically. Yet the core challenges of human life remain much the same. People still wrestle with questions of identity, families still struggle with loyalty, jealousy, and reconciliation, communities still debate how power should be used, and individuals still face decisions that test integrity and trust.

Genesis invites readers to examine these patterns through the lens of ancient stories that continue to illuminate modern experience.

The purpose of this book is to guide readers through Genesis with clarity and context. Rather than assuming specialized theological knowledge, the following chapters walk step by step through the narrative, exploring its historical background, its central themes, and its relevance for contemporary life.

The structure of this book reflects that goal. The opening chapter considers the fundamental human question Genesis addresses: why the world appears both beautiful and broken. Readers are then introduced to the historical environment in which the book emerged, because understanding the geography, cultural practices, and political structures of the ancient Near East provides essential context for interpreting the stories.

From there, the narrative of Genesis itself is explored in detail, tracing the movement of the story from creation to the formation of a single family through whom a larger promise begins to unfold. Subsequent chapters examine the key themes that appear throughout the book, clarify common misunderstandings, and consider how the insights of Genesis continue to speak to modern situations involving leadership, relationships, decision-making, and personal integrity. The book concludes with reflections and questions designed to help readers engage the text more personally.

Genesis is often described as a book of beginnings. It introduces the origin of the universe, the beginnings of human society, and the early history of families whose descendants will shape the rest of the biblical narrative. But perhaps most importantly, Genesis marks the beginning of a story that addresses one of humanity's most enduring questions.

If the world is broken, can it be restored?

The chapters that follow explore how Genesis begins to answer that question.

Chapter 1

The Human Question

The woman sees that the tree's fruit looks good for food, appealing to the eye, and desirable for gaining wisdom. She takes some, eats it, and gives some to her husband, who is with her, and he eats it too. Then their eyes are opened, and they suddenly realize they are naked. They sew fig leaves together and make coverings for themselves.
—Genesis 3:6-7 (NIV)

Why Is the World Broken?

Every generation eventually confronts the same difficult question: **Why is the world broken?**

The question rarely appears all at once. It usually begins quietly. A child notices injustice for the first time. Someone is treated unfairly at school. A friend betrays a promise. A tragedy appears on the evening news. In those moments a simple observation begins to form something about the world is not as it should be.

As people grow older, the question deepens. Adults encounter loss, disappointment, and betrayal. Relationships that once seemed secure begin to fracture. Careers that promised fulfillment sometimes leave a lingering sense of emptiness. Communities struggle with division, and entire nations wrestle with conflict and instability.

Over time many people reach the same realization: despite remarkable advances in knowledge and technology, humanity continues to struggle with the same fundamental problems.

The world changes, but the human condition often does not.

History reveals this tension again and again. Civilizations rise with hopes of justice and stability, only to encounter corruption and conflict. Political systems promise reform yet often repeat the same patterns of power and abuse that existed in previous generations. Families build legacies of strength and love, but they also carry unresolved wounds that echo from one generation to the next.

Individuals pursue success, recognition, and influence. Many achieve remarkable accomplishments. Yet even those who reach positions of power or wealth often discover that achievement alone does not answer the deeper questions of identity and purpose. Human progress is real, but it is incomplete.

A World That Advances—And Yet Remains the Same

Over the last century, technological advancement has reshaped the modern world in extraordinary ways. Cities have expanded into vast networks of commerce and culture. Digital communication now travels across continents in seconds. Medical science has extended life expectancy and alleviated diseases that once devastated entire populations.

Scientific discoveries continue to reveal the complexity of the universe, offering insights that previous generations could scarcely imagine. Satellites orbit the earth, spacecraft explore distant planets, and artificial intelligence processes information at astonishing speeds. Human ingenuity is remarkable.

Yet beneath these extraordinary achievements lies a deeper reality that technology alone cannot fix. The inner struggles of human nature remain remarkably consistent. Pride still damages relationships, fear still shapes decisions, and jealousy still drives conflict. Greed influences the pursuit of wealth and power, while ambition can inspire innovation and leadership but also tempt individuals to sacrifice integrity in order to achieve success.

Communities wrestle with ethical dilemmas that mirror those faced by societies thousands of years ago. Institutions struggle to balance power with responsibility, and families navigate conflicts that feel as old as humanity itself. The tools have changed, but human nature has not changed nearly as much.

The Ancient Question

Long before modern technology, long before global communication and digital networks, ancient societies were already wrestling with the same questions.

Why do people hurt one another?

Why do communities drift toward conflict?

Why does the world contain both extraordinary beauty and profound suffering?

The book of Genesis begins by confronting these questions directly. Rather than starting with religious rules or philosophical arguments, Genesis begins with origins. It explores the foundations of human existence through narrative, asking where humanity came from and why the world reflects both dignity and brokenness.

Genesis approaches these questions not through abstract theory but through story. It tells the story of beginnings—the beginning of the physical universe, the beginning of human relationships, and the beginning of the struggles that continue to shape history. The book does not merely explain events; it reveals patterns.

A World Created with Purpose

The opening chapters of Genesis describe a universe created with intention and order. In contrast to many ancient myths that portrayed the world emerging from chaos or violent conflict among competing gods, Genesis presents creation as the result of purposeful design.

Light separates from darkness. Land rises from the seas. Vegetation spreads across the earth. Animals fill the sky, the land, and the waters.

Each stage of creation unfolds with deliberate structure. The narrative moves with rhythm and clarity, describing a world that emerges not from disorder but from purposeful action. Humanity appears as the final act of creation, and the world begins in harmony.

Creation functions as it was intended. The natural world flourishes, and human beings live within that world with purpose and responsibility. The relationship between humanity and the rest of creation reflects balance rather than exploitation.

At the center of this newly formed world stands humanity itself.

Identity Before Accomplishment

Within this newly formed creation, human beings receive a unique role. Genesis describes humanity as being made in the image of God, a phrase that suggests both dignity and responsibility.

Human life carries inherent value not because of power, wealth, intelligence, or achievement, but because of the relationship between humanity and its Creator. Identity comes before accomplishment.

This idea was radical in the ancient world. In many societies a person's worth depended almost entirely on social status. Kings and elites were often viewed as superior to ordinary people, while those without power were easily dismissed or ignored.

Genesis offers a different starting point: every human life carries dignity because every person reflects something of the Creator.

This principle reshapes the foundation of human identity. Value does not depend on social class, wealth, education, or influence. Instead, dignity originates from creation itself, meaning human worth begins with being rather than merely with doing.

Responsibility and Stewardship

This dignity is paired with responsibility. Genesis portrays humanity as stewards of creation, entrusted with cultivating and caring for the world rather than exploiting it. The relationship between humanity and the natural world is intended to be cooperative rather than destructive.

People are not simply inhabitants of the world; they are caretakers of it.

This responsibility extends beyond environmental stewardship. It includes the way people treat one another, build communities, and shape cultures. The authority given to humanity is not meant to produce domination or control but to encourage care, cultivation, and responsibility.

Yet this responsibility also includes something remarkable: freedom.

The Risk of Freedom

Genesis portrays human beings as moral agents capable of making real decisions. The first humans are not described as passive participants in a predetermined system. Instead, they possess the ability to respond to God with trust or rebellion.

Freedom allows for creativity, growth, and meaningful relationships, but it also introduces risk. Without freedom, love and trust would be meaningless. Yet with freedom comes the possibility of choosing wrongly. The capacity to act with wisdom also includes the capacity to act with selfishness.

Genesis does not ignore this reality. Instead, it places it at the center of the story.

The Turning Point

The turning point of Genesis occurs when the first humans encounter a boundary placed within the garden where they live. The boundary is simple, representing a test of trust rather than an arbitrary restriction.

The question is not about fruit. The question is about trust— whether humanity will rely on the wisdom of the Creator or attempt to define good and evil independently.

The decision arrives quietly. They choose independence.

At first the moment appears small: a single act of disobedience within a garden. Yet the consequences ripple outward through every generation that follows. The garden is lost, relationships fracture, shame enters the human experience, and fear replaces openness. Violence appears within the first family, and entire societies eventually drift toward corruption and injustice.

Harmony gives way to struggle.

A World of Beauty and Brokenness

Genesis explains why the world often feels divided between beauty and brokenness. The world still reflects the order and creativity of its Creator. Mountains rise above valleys, oceans stretch across continents, and human beings continue to create art, build communities, and pursue justice.

Beauty remains.

But brokenness remains as well.

The tension between these two realities shapes human experience. People long for peace yet often contribute to conflict. Communities strive for justice yet repeatedly encounter corruption. Families pursue love and loyalty but sometimes fracture under the weight of jealousy, pride, or misunderstanding.

Genesis recognizes this complexity. The story does not pretend that the world is either entirely good or entirely hopeless. Instead, it reveals how both beauty and brokenness exist simultaneously within the human experience.

The Persistence of Grace

Yet Genesis does not present a narrative of despair. Alongside the failures of humanity, another theme quietly emerges throughout the story: the persistence of grace.

Moments of judgment are often followed by unexpected mercy. Even when individuals make destructive choices, the possibility of restoration continues to appear. Noah survives the flood, Abraham receives a promise, Jacob encounters transformation, and Joseph forgives the brothers who betrayed him.

Failure is not the end of the story.

The narrative repeatedly suggests that even when human beings move in destructive directions, the possibility of redemption remains open.

Questions That Still Matter

Genesis raises questions that remain deeply relevant for modern readers.

Why do human relationships fracture so easily, even among people who care deeply for one another?

Why does success sometimes arrive with moral compromise?

Why do families often repeat patterns of conflict across generations?

These questions are not theoretical. They appear in everyday life. A leader faces pressure to compromise integrity in order to achieve results. A family struggles with resentment that has been quietly building for years. An individual wrestles with the tension between ambition and conscience.

Genesis recognizes that these struggles are not new. The people who appear in its pages lived in tents and traveled across deserts rather than modern cities, yet their motivations and fears remain strikingly familiar. They wrestle with loyalty and insecurity, struggle with faith and doubt, and experience both courage and failure.

Deeply Human Characters

The characters in Genesis are not idealized heroes. They are deeply human.

Abraham struggles with fear when confronting powerful rulers. Jacob manipulates circumstances in order to gain advantage over his brother. Joseph's brothers allow jealousy to grow until it leads to betrayal. Their failures are not hidden; they are part of the story.

This honesty is one of the reasons Genesis continues to resonate across centuries. Readers recognize something of themselves in the individuals who populate its pages. The narrative reflects the complexities of human nature rather than presenting an unrealistic portrait of perfection.

People see their own struggles reflected in the story.

The Direction of the Story

Yet through these flawed individuals, a larger pattern gradually becomes visible. Even in the midst of human weakness, movement toward restoration continues. Lives shaped by failure can still be redirected toward transformation. Broken relationships sometimes move toward reconciliation, and moments of suffering occasionally lead to unexpected purpose.

Redemption remains possible.

Genesis serves as more than a historical introduction to the Bible. It provides a framework for understanding the human condition itself. The book explains why the world contains both beauty and brokenness while also suggesting that history is moving toward something more than chaos.

The problem is real, but so is the promise.

Genesis is not simply a story about the beginning of the world. It is a story about the beginning of hope—a hope that unfolds gradually through the lives of imperfect people and through the unfolding relationship between humanity and its Creator.

The questions raised in Genesis continue to echo across every generation.

Because every generation eventually asks them.

Chapter 2

Orientation

In the beginning, God created the heavens and the earth.
—Genesis 1:1

Understanding the Role of Genesis

Genesis stands at the very beginning of the Bible, serving as the opening text of a collection known as the Pentateuch. The Pentateuch includes the first five books of Scripture—Genesis, Exodus, Leviticus, Numbers, and Deuteronomy—and together they establish the foundation upon which the rest of the biblical story is built. These books introduce the central themes, relationships, and historical movements that shape everything that follows in Scripture. They function like the opening briefing before a long operation: they establish where we are, why it matters, what went wrong, and what must be done moving forward.

Genesis is the first voice in that sequence, and it sets the tone for the entire narrative. It explains how the world began, why humanity is both glorious and fractured, and how God's plan moves forward even when people fail. In that sense, Genesis is not only a beginning in terms of chronology. It is a beginning in terms of meaning. It teaches readers how to interpret everything that follows by laying down the categories that the rest of Scripture assumes you already understand.

The name "Genesis" comes from a Greek word meaning origin or beginning, a title that captures the purpose of the book with remarkable accuracy. Genesis is fundamentally a book about beginnings. It explores the origins of the universe, the emergence of humanity, the first appearance of sin, and the early development of the family that will eventually become the nation of Israel. It also establishes the roots of human identity, human conflict, and human longing. In these opening pages, readers encounter the starting point of the biblical narrative, and they begin to see that the Bible is not merely a collection of moral lessons. It is a story—one long, unfolding account of creation, fracture, promise, and restoration.

Without Genesis, the rest of the Bible would be extraordinarily difficult to understand. Later books repeatedly refer back to events, promises, and ideas first introduced here. They assume you know what the covenant is, why it matters, and why the world needs redemption in the first place. Even the language of faith, sin, blessing, judgment, mercy, and deliverance makes far less sense without the backdrop that Genesis provides.

Among the most important ideas introduced in Genesis are the concepts of creation, human dignity, rebellion, judgment, mercy, covenant, and redemption. These are not side themes. They are structural beams. They hold up the whole building. Later books revisit them again and again—sometimes expanding on them, sometimes wrestling with them, sometimes correcting distortions of them—but always assuming that the reader understands their original context. Genesis, therefore, does more than begin the Bible chronologically. It provides the interpretive framework through which everything else must be understood, introducing the central tension between human freedom and divine purpose, a tension that will continue throughout the biblical story.

The Question of Authorship

Traditionally, Genesis has been attributed to Moses. According to long-standing Jewish and Christian belief, Moses compiled and recorded the material contained in the Pentateuch during the early formation of Israel as a nation. This view reflects the role Moses plays throughout the early books of the Bible as both a leader and a teacher responsible for guiding the people of Israel through a period of profound transition.

Moses lived during a pivotal moment in Israel's history. After centuries of slavery in Egypt, the descendants of Abraham were emerging as a distinct people under God's leadership. They were no longer simply an extended family or tribal group. They were becoming a nation with shared identity, shared memory, and shared purpose. That shift matters because nations are not sustained on geography alone. They are sustained on story. They need a shared understanding of where they came from, why they exist, and what they are called to become.

In this context, Genesis functions as a historical and theological introduction for the people of Israel. The stories contained in the book explain where the nation came from, reminding the people of the covenant promises made to their ancestors. The narratives also place Israel's story within the broader story of humanity, connecting the experiences of a single family to the larger human condition. It is as if Genesis says, "Your story didn't begin in Egypt. It didn't begin with Pharaoh. It didn't begin with your trauma. It began long before that, and what you're living through is part of a much bigger account."

The earliest events described in Genesis reach far beyond the lifetime of Moses. The narratives of creation, the flood, and the early patriarchs take place in a distant past that precedes written historical records. Yet the final form of the text likely emerged during the second millennium BCE as these traditions were gathered, preserved, and organized into the narrative that readers encounter today. Genesis reflects both ancient memory and theological reflection. It tells stories rooted in the distant past while also addressing the needs of a people learning to understand their identity. The book serves as a bridge between early human history and the emerging national story of Israel, giving them context for their suffering and meaning for their future.

The Foundation of the Biblical Story

To appreciate the importance of Genesis, it helps to imagine reading the Bible without it. If you remove Genesis, you do not simply lose the beginning. You lose the lens. You lose the reason the rest of the story exists.

Without Genesis, readers would encounter a people called Israel without knowing where they came from. They would encounter references to a covenant without knowing when or why that covenant was established. They would hear about sin, redemption, sacrifice, and divine promises without understanding the original circumstances that created the need for those ideas. You would hear about deliverance in Exodus without understanding why people needed deliverance in the first place. You would read about law and worship without understanding why humanity requires guidance, boundaries, and reconciliation.

Genesis provides the missing context. It answers foundational questions that shape the rest of Scripture. It explains where humanity comes from, why the world contains suffering and conflict, and why God chooses to work through a particular family in order to address the brokenness of the world. These questions are not simply theological curiosities. They form the narrative foundation upon which the entire biblical story rests.

Every major theme introduced later in Scripture—whether in the historical books, the prophetic writings, or the teachings of the New Testament—can be traced back to concepts first introduced in Genesis. The story of deliverance traces back to slavery and promise. The story of sacrifice traces back to human guilt and divine mercy. The story of redemption traces back to the fracture in Eden and the promise to Abraham.

Genesis establishes the setting for the entire Bible. It introduces the central problem of human rebellion and the initial promise that restoration will eventually come. Everything else builds from there.

Two Movements Within the Book

Although Genesis covers an enormous span of time, the structure of the book is surprisingly clear. The narrative unfolds in two major movements, each with a distinct focus. The first movement addresses the story of humanity as a whole. The second movement narrows the focus to one family through whom God begins to address the brokenness of the world. Together, these two movements explain both the problem and the promise that shape the rest of Scripture.

This structure matters because it reveals how Genesis thinks about restoration. It begins by showing that humanity, left to itself, cannot stabilize the world. The breakdown is too deep and too widespread. Then it shows that God's response is not merely to issue commands from a distance. God moves toward people. He calls, promises, guides, corrects, and preserves—often working through messy human lives to accomplish something larger than any one person can see.

The First Movement: Humanity's Story

The opening eleven chapters of Genesis describe the early history of the human race. These chapters explore the origin of the world, the creation of humanity, and the introduction of sin into human experience. The narrative begins with creation itself. God forms the heavens and the earth, establishes order within the universe, and creates humanity in his image. The opening chapter presents a world that begins in harmony, where creation reflects purpose and balance.

Yet that harmony does not last long.

The story of the fall introduces rebellion into the human story. Adam and Eve choose independence over trust, and their decision alters the trajectory of human history. Shame, conflict, and suffering enter the world, changing the relationship between humanity, nature, and God. From that moment forward, Genesis presents sin not merely as wrongdoing but as a rupture— something that fractures trust, distorts identity, and spreads outward.

The consequences spread quickly. The next generation witnesses the first murder as Cain kills his brother Abel out of jealousy. Violence begins to multiply within human society as resentment, pride, and rivalry shape relationships between individuals and communities. The narrative suggests that evil does not remain contained. It spreads like a contaminant through families and cultures. People build cities, develop skills, create systems of life—and the same systems become channels for corruption as often as they become channels for flourishing.

Eventually, corruption becomes so widespread that the narrative describes the world as filled with destructive behavior. The flood represents a dramatic moment of judgment and renewal, confronting the moral collapse of human society while preserving life through Noah and his family. In that story, readers see both severity and mercy: the seriousness of human corruption and the determination of God to preserve a future.

Even after this new beginning, humanity continues to struggle with pride and ambition. The story of the Tower of Babel illustrates humanity's desire to establish identity and power apart from God. The builders attempt to create a monument to their own achievements, seeking unity and recognition on their own terms. Their project is not merely construction. It is self-salvation. It is the attempt to secure meaning through human effort alone.

The result is confusion and scattering. Language is disrupted, and communities disperse across the earth. This first section of

Genesis describes a pattern that remains recognizable throughout human history: creation is followed by rebellion, and rebellion leads to the spread of corruption. Human societies repeatedly struggle with the tension between responsibility and ambition. By the end of these chapters, the central problem has become clear: humanity cannot repair the world on its own.

The Second Movement: The Story of One Family

Beginning in chapter twelve, the focus of Genesis shifts dramatically. Instead of tracing the story of humanity as a whole, the narrative concentrates on a single individual named Abraham. This shift marks a turning point in the biblical narrative. Rather than attempting to address the entire human race directly, God begins working through one family.

Abraham receives a call that will shape the rest of Scripture. He is instructed to leave his homeland and travel to a destination that has not yet been revealed. The journey requires extraordinary trust, since Abraham must abandon familiar surroundings without knowing exactly where the path will lead. This is not a small request in an ancient world where security was tied to land, kin, and clan. Leaving meant vulnerability. It meant risk. It meant surrendering control.

God promises that Abraham will become the father of a great nation and that through his descendants the entire world will ultimately be blessed. This promise becomes known as the covenant with Abraham, one of the most significant developments in the entire Bible. It introduces a central theme: God does not abandon humanity after rebellion. He initiates a path toward restoration.

From this point forward, the narrative follows the lives of four key figures whose experiences shape the identity of the future nation of Israel: Abraham, Isaac, Jacob, and Joseph.

Each of these individuals represents a stage in the unfolding promise. Abraham receives the covenant and begins the journey of faith. Isaac inherits the promise and continues the family line. Jacob becomes the father of the twelve tribes of Israel, establishing the structure of the future nation. Joseph ultimately preserves the family during a devastating famine, ensuring that the covenant line survives.

Through their lives, the narrative explores the complexities of faith, family relationships, and leadership. None of these individuals is presented as a flawless hero. Abraham struggles with fear. Jacob manipulates circumstances to gain an advantage over his brother. Joseph's brothers allow jealousy to grow until it leads to betrayal. What makes Genesis compelling is that God's plan moves forward in the middle of that human reality, not after it has been cleaned up.

Yet through these complicated lives, the covenant continues to move forward. The story reveals a remarkable truth about the unfolding biblical narrative: God's purposes often advance through imperfect people and unpredictable circumstances. The promise persists even when human behavior fails.

Preparing for the Story of Exodus

The final chapters of Genesis lead directly into the events described in the book of Exodus. Joseph rises to power in Egypt after interpreting Pharaoh's dreams and preparing the nation for a coming famine. When famine spreads across the surrounding regions, Joseph's family travels to Egypt seeking food.

What begins as a desperate journey eventually becomes a turning point in the biblical story.

Joseph forgives his brothers and invites the entire family to settle in Egypt, where they are given land and protection. For a time, the family prospers, growing in number and influence within the Egyptian territory. This move preserves the family, but it also creates the conditions for the next crisis. People living under protection can eventually become people living under threat. A welcomed family can eventually become an enslaved population.

Genesis ends with an unresolved tension. The descendants of Abraham are living in a foreign land. They have not yet become the nation that God promised, and the covenant remains active but incomplete. The story pauses at this moment in history. The next chapter of the narrative will reveal what happens when the descendants of Abraham grow into a large population within Egypt. Over time, they will lose their freedom and become enslaved, setting the stage for the dramatic events that unfold in the book of Exodus.

The Purpose of Genesis

Genesis does more than introduce historical events. It prepares readers to understand the larger narrative of the Bible by explaining the origin of humanity, the emergence of sin, and the introduction of God's plan to restore what has been broken.

The book establishes the problem that defines human history while also introducing the promise that restoration will eventually come. From the creation of the world to the preservation of a single family in Egypt, Genesis lays the groundwork for everything that follows. It shows that the world is broken, why it is broken, and how God begins to move toward restoration—not through instant force, but through covenant, promise, and patient purpose.

The story that begins in Genesis will continue to unfold across the pages of Scripture, revealing how the tension between brokenness and redemption develops through generations of human history.

And in Genesis, that story is only beginning.

Chapter 3

The World Behind the Book

*That is why it was called Babel, because there the Lord confused
the language of the whole world. From there,
the Lord scattered them over the face of the whole earth.*
—Genesis 11:9

Understanding the world in which Genesis unfolds helps modern readers see the stories with greater clarity. At first glance, the events described in the book may feel distant. They take place thousands of years ago in landscapes that many modern readers have never seen and within cultures that operated according to very different assumptions about society, religion, and identity. The names can sound foreign, the travel patterns can feel slow, and the family structures can seem complicated. But once the historical and cultural environment behind Genesis becomes clearer, many of the narratives begin to make far more sense. The movements of the patriarchs, the tensions within families, and the religious ideas presented throughout the book all emerge from a particular setting in time and place.

Genesis unfolds primarily in a region historians refer to as the ancient Near East. This broad area includes much of modern-day Iraq, Syria, Israel, Jordan, and Egypt. It was one of the earliest centers of human civilization and the birthplace of some of the world's first cities, political systems, and trade networks. This matters because Genesis is not written in a vacuum. The book is telling a story about real people living inside real cultural pressures—pressures involving survival, honor, power, fertility, land, and lineage. When you understand those pressures, the decisions of the characters become easier to interpret. You start to see that what looks like "random travel" is often strategic movement. What looks like "family drama" is often a fight over inheritance, authority, and survival. What looks like "religious language" is often an intentional contrast with the dominant beliefs of surrounding nations.

Early Civilization and the Birthplace of Cities

Civilization in this region did not appear suddenly. It developed gradually along fertile river valleys where agriculture became possible. Communities that once depended primarily on hunting and gathering began to settle in places where crops could be cultivated reliably and where water sources allowed livestock to flourish. With stable food supplies came larger populations. With larger populations came specialization—farmers, craftsmen, traders, builders, administrators, and rulers. Over time, villages expanded into towns and eventually into cities.

Two of the most important rivers in this region were the Tigris and Euphrates. These rivers flowed through a land known as Mesopotamia, a name that literally means "the land between the rivers." The fertile soil along these waterways allowed early agricultural societies to flourish, and that fertility created economic surplus. Surplus is what allows societies to build. It allows for storage, planning, record-keeping, and defense. It also creates the conditions for power—because whoever controls surplus controls life.

It was here that some of the earliest urban societies in human history appeared. Cities such as Ur, Babylon, and Nineveh grew into centers of commerce, culture, and political authority. Long before the events described in the later books of the Bible, these cities were already thriving hubs where farmers, merchants, craftsmen, and rulers interacted within complex social systems. Trade connected these urban centers to distant regions, bringing metals, textiles, livestock, and grain into bustling marketplaces.

Roads and river routes became lifelines. Markets became meeting points where language, customs, and religious ideas mixed.

Writing systems began to develop in these environments as well. Clay tablets preserved records of trade agreements, laws, religious rituals, and administrative decisions. Organized governments emerged to manage growing populations, defend territories, and regulate economic activity. In many ways, these cities looked like early versions of what modern people would recognize as organized society: leadership hierarchies, courts, taxation, religious institutions, and economic stratification. There were elites and laborers, protected insiders and vulnerable outsiders.

Within this broader world of early civilization, Genesis situates the beginnings of the biblical story. That is important because Genesis is not trying to tell you that the ancient world was primitive and simple. It's telling you that even in sophisticated societies—places with commerce, law, and religion—human beings still wrestled with pride, fear, envy, deception, and violence. Progress existed. Brokenness existed, too.

Ur and the Starting Point of Abraham's Journey

One of these cities, Ur, holds particular significance for the narrative of Genesis. According to the text, Abraham—the central figure in the second half of the book—begins his journey there. Archaeological discoveries suggest that Ur was a prosperous and sophisticated urban center during the early second millennium BCE. The city contained large temples dedicated to regional deities, extensive residential areas, and active trading networks that connected Mesopotamia with surrounding regions. Its inhabitants practiced agriculture, developed systems of accounting, and participated in organized civic life.

In other words, Abraham did not begin his life in an isolated desert village. He began in a sophisticated civilization shaped by commerce, religion, and political organization. This detail changes how you read the call of Abraham. Leaving Ur is not simply "moving somewhere else." It is walking away from stability. It is stepping out of a predictable system where protection, identity, and economic opportunity are tied to city life and family networks.

Recognizing this background helps readers understand the magnitude of Abraham's later decision when he leaves his homeland in response to God's call. The journey described in Genesis is not merely a relocation to another place. It represents a profound departure from the security and familiarity of a well-established society. Leaving Ur meant leaving behind economic stability, social structure, predictable alliances, and the protection offered by a powerful city. Abraham steps away from that stability and travels toward a future that is largely unknown, carrying only a promise and the responsibility of leading a household through uncertainty.

In the ancient world, this is not a casual risk. It is a life-altering exposure. The farther you move from established networks, the more vulnerable you become—to famine, conflict, exploitation, and isolation. Abraham's journey reads not only as spiritual obedience, but as a high-stakes act of trust in a world where trust can get people killed.

Geography and Movement

The geography of the ancient Near East also played an important role in shaping how people lived and traveled. Unlike the modern world, where paved roads, vehicles, and communication networks connect distant regions, travel in the ancient world required careful preparation and patience. Journeys were slow and exposed. They demanded planning for water, food, animals, and safe routes. The environment itself shaped strategy.

Journeys often followed natural pathways shaped by rivers, valleys, and seasonal weather patterns. Travelers avoided harsh desert terrain whenever possible, choosing routes that provided access to water and grazing land for animals. Caravans of traders and travelers moved along established routes that linked the great civilizations of the region. One of the most important trade corridors stretched from Mesopotamia in the east to Egypt in the southwest. This route passed through the land later known as Canaan, a region that would eventually become central to the story of Israel.

Merchants traveling along these roads transported a wide range of goods. Grain, textiles, metals, spices, pottery, and livestock moved between cities and settlements. Trade networks allowed distant cultures to interact economically while also exchanging ideas and beliefs. When people travel, they don't only move products. They move the worldview. They bring stories, fears, gods, and politics with them.

Cultural influences traveled along the same paths as material goods. Languages spread across regions. Religious traditions influenced neighboring communities. Political alliances formed and dissolved as leaders negotiated access to trade routes and resources. A drought in one region could drive migration into another. A new king could shift trade policy overnight. A famine could turn peace into conflict quickly.

Movement was therefore a normal part of life in this environment. Migration was common, particularly among groups that depended on livestock. Families and tribal groups often relocated in search of grazing land, fresh water, or economic opportunity. These migrations could be seasonal or long-term depending on environmental conditions. The journeys described throughout Genesis—from Abraham's travels across Canaan to Jacob's migrations with his family—fit naturally within this cultural setting. They are not random wanderings. They are survival decisions made in response to land, weather, conflict, and opportunity.

Nomadic and semi-nomadic lifestyles were widespread across the region. Many extended families lived in tents and moved with their flocks of sheep and goats according to seasonal patterns of pasture and rainfall. During certain times of the year, they settled temporarily near towns or agricultural regions, trading animal products for grain and other supplies. Shepherding and herding required constant attention. It also required negotiation with settled communities, because pastureland, wells, and territory were not unlimited. This helps explain why disputes over wells, land boundaries, and grazing rights appear repeatedly in the patriarchal narratives. In a dry region, a well is not just a convenience. It is life.

This mobility explains why the patriarchs in Genesis appear frequently on the move. Their lives reflect the rhythms of a world where mobility was not unusual but necessary for survival, and where a family's future could depend on the ability to relocate at the right time.

The Importance of Family and Clan

One of the most important differences between the ancient world and modern societies lies in the way identity was understood. In many contemporary cultures, individuals often define themselves through personal achievements, careers, education, or personal choices. Success and identity are frequently framed as individual accomplishments. People ask, "What do you do?" and "What have you achieved?" as the main measures of significance.

In the ancient Near East, identity worked very differently. A person's primary identity came from belonging to a family or clan. Your name was not just personal. It was connected. Your future was not primarily individual. It was communal. The family was the first system of protection, the first economy, the first legal defense, and the first social safety net.

Family structures were large, interconnected systems that included multiple generations. A typical household might consist of parents, children, grandparents, servants, and extended relatives living together or in close proximity. These networks formed the basic unit of social organization. They also formed the basic unit of survival. Without a family network, a person had little protection in a world without modern police, insurance, or courts that guaranteed equal treatment.

Because of this structure, the actions of one individual could influence the reputation and well-being of the entire group. Honor and shame were powerful social forces. Maintaining the stability and reputation of the family was often considered more important than pursuing personal ambition. A public disgrace could weaken a family's ability to negotiate marriages, trade agreements, and alliances. A broken relationship could become a long-term vulnerability.

This cultural framework helps explain many of the tensions that appear throughout Genesis. Sibling rivalry becomes especially intense when inheritance and leadership within the family are involved. Inheritance determined not only wealth but also authority, influence, and the continuation of family leadership. The "firstborn" concept was not a sentimental tradition. It was governance. It was succession.

Conflicts between brothers—such as Cain and Abel, Jacob and Esau, or Joseph and his siblings—therefore carried consequences far beyond personal disagreement. These disputes affected the future structure and stability of the entire family. They were struggles over inheritance, authority, and the direction of the clan. When you understand that, you read these stories with more gravity. The betrayals are not petty. They are existential.

Understanding this dynamic helps readers recognize why family relationships dominate so much of the narrative. Genesis is not simply telling a collection of individual stories. It is tracing the development of a lineage through which the biblical promise will eventually unfold. The future of the family matters deeply within the story because the future of the promise depends on it, and the promise itself is carried forward through births, marriages, blessings, and inheritances.

Religion in the Ancient World

Religion played an equally central role in the societies of the ancient Near East. Nearly every civilization in the region believed that the natural world was governed by a complex system of divine beings and spiritual forces. Most of these religious systems were polytheistic, meaning that people worshiped multiple gods.

Different deities were associated with different aspects of life and nature. Some gods were believed to control storms, fertility, or harvests. Others governed the sun, moon, rivers, or seasonal cycles. Individual cities often had patron gods thought to protect their inhabitants and ensure prosperity. This meant religion was often local. A god could be tied to a place. A shrine could be tied to a territory. In many cultures, to leave a land meant leaving the protection of that land's god.

Temples were constructed to honor these deities, and priests performed rituals designed to maintain the favor of the gods. Sacrifices, offerings, and festivals were common expressions of devotion intended to secure blessings or prevent disaster. People did not only worship out of gratitude. They worshiped out of fear. They sought stability in a world filled with drought, disease, childbirth danger, and war.

Religion in this world was not merely a private belief system. It shaped the entire structure of society. Political authority was often closely tied to religious legitimacy. Kings claimed the support of particular gods, and military victories were sometimes interpreted as signs of divine approval. Agricultural success or failure could also be understood as evidence of divine favor or judgment.

Against this cultural background, the God described in Genesis appears remarkably different. The biblical narrative does not describe a god associated with a particular river, mountain, or city. Instead, Genesis introduces a Creator who stands above creation itself. This God creates the universe rather than emerging from it. This God speaks the world into existence rather than battling rival deities. This God governs not merely one nation but the entire cosmos.

For audiences familiar with polytheistic traditions, this perspective would have been strikingly different from the religious assumptions surrounding them. Genesis presents a radically distinct vision of reality: one Creator, one authority, one source of life. That claim is not merely theological. It is confrontational. It challenges the dominant map of how the world works.

A Personal Relationship

Another distinctive feature of Genesis is the personal nature of God's interaction with humanity. In many ancient religions, the gods were believed to be distant or unpredictable, concerned primarily with maintaining cosmic balance rather than forming relationships with human beings. People attempted to appease these deities through rituals and sacrifices in hopes of avoiding catastrophe or gaining favor.

In Genesis, however, God interacts with people in direct and personal ways. God speaks to Adam and Eve in the garden, addressing them after their disobedience. God warns Cain about the destructive potential of unchecked anger before violence occurs. God calls Abraham to leave his homeland and promises to bless his descendants through a covenant relationship. God engages Jacob in a moment of struggle that leaves him changed.

God stays with Joseph through betrayal, slavery, and prison, positioning him for leadership in a foreign land.

These encounters portray a relationship that is both personal and purposeful. God is not distant or indifferent to human affairs. Instead, the narrative repeatedly emphasizes communication between the Creator and individuals, suggesting that human history unfolds within the context of an ongoing relationship between God and humanity. The direction of the story is shaped not merely by political events but by divine initiative and human response.

This concept would have challenged many of the assumptions present in ancient religious thought. It continues to challenge readers today because it refuses to reduce faith to ritual alone. Genesis presents faith as relational trust, obedience, and dependence in the middle of real life.

A Decentralized Political World

The political environment reflected in Genesis also differs significantly from the massive empires that dominate later biblical history. During the period reflected in Genesis, the ancient Near East was largely organized around city-states and regional kingdoms. Instead of large, centralized empires controlling vast territories, power was distributed among numerous smaller rulers who governed individual cities and surrounding lands.

These kings controlled relatively limited areas of territory and often competed with neighboring rulers for resources, trade routes, and influence. Alliances formed and dissolved frequently, and political stability could shift quickly as conflicts erupted between rival leaders. This was a world where treaties were fragile, where raids could happen, and where local rulers might demand tribute or attempt to exploit traveling groups.

Because political authority was fragmented, borders were often fluid. This decentralized structure created a world where families and tribal groups could move across regions without encountering the rigid territorial boundaries associated with later imperial systems. Families could migrate in search of water, pasture, or economic opportunity without necessarily facing the restrictions imposed by powerful centralized governments. That said, mobility did not mean safety. Moving into another territory could expose a family to suspicion, exploitation, or conflict with local rulers.

This political environment helps explain how figures like Abraham and Jacob were able to travel significant distances with their households and livestock. Their movements were consistent with the realities of a world where pastoral communities regularly moved between territories as environmental conditions required. It also helps explain why Genesis includes moments where patriarchs interact with kings, negotiate agreements, and attempt to protect their families through strategic decisions—sometimes honorable, sometimes fearful, sometimes both.

A Different Way of Seeing the World

When readers step back and consider this cultural background, the book of Genesis begins to appear even more remarkable. It emerges from a world shaped by polytheistic religion, clan-based identity, and decentralized political structures. Yet within that environment, the narrative introduces a radically different way of understanding reality.

Genesis presents a universe governed by one Creator rather than many competing gods. It describes human beings as carrying inherent dignity because they are created in the image of God. It suggests that history is not a random sequence of events but part of a larger story moving toward purpose. It does not deny the reality of human failure, violence, and corruption, but it refuses to conclude that these things are final.

These ideas challenged many of the assumptions that defined ancient culture. They continue to challenge readers today. Genesis does not simply record historical events. It introduces a framework for understanding existence itself—a perspective that will shape the unfolding story of Scripture and influence generations of readers who encounter its narrative.

And from this world—real places, real pressures, real human conflict—the story of Genesis moves forward, setting the foundation for everything that follows.

Chapter 4

The Story or Flow of the Book

*The Lord had said to Abram, "Go from your country, your people
and your father's household to the land I will show you." I will
make you into a great nation, and I will bless you; I will make
your name great, and you will be a blessing
—Genesis 12:1-2*

Genesis unfolds as a sweeping narrative that moves from the creation of the universe to the formation of a single family through whom God intends to restore what humanity has broken. The book covers an enormous span of time and moves across multiple regions of the ancient world, yet beneath the movement of events, the story follows a clear and deliberate progression. It begins with the world itself and then traces what happens when human beings step out of trust and into self-rule.

Genesis moves like a river. The scenes change, generations come and go, and the geography shifts, but a consistent pattern remains. The book begins with creation and blessing, moves into rebellion and fracture, and then narrows toward covenant and promise. The first half explains the human problem on a universal scale. The second half introduces the beginning of a long-term solution through one chosen family.

Understanding this progression helps readers see how the stories connect. Genesis is not a random collection of ancient traditions. It is a carefully arranged narrative that moves from universal beginnings toward a particular promise, and it does so with remarkable psychological realism. The characters do not live in a simplified moral world. They live in the same kind of world modern readers recognize: a world where fear influences decisions, where relationships break under pressure, and where hope can still emerge from failure.

Creation: Order from Chaos

Genesis opens with one of the most recognizable sentences in all of literature: "In the beginning, God created the heavens and the earth." The statement is brief, yet its implications are enormous. Before anything existed—before the stars, the oceans, the mountains, or humanity itself—God already was. The universe does not arise from a struggle between rival gods or from chaotic cosmic forces. Instead, creation begins with intention and design.

The opening chapter describes the formation of the world in a series of ordered stages. Light appears first, separating day from night and establishing the rhythm of time. The sky emerges, dividing waters above from waters below. Land rises from the seas, providing a place where life can flourish. Vegetation spreads across the earth, and then the sun, moon, and stars appear in the heavens to mark seasons and cycles. Birds fill the air and fish populate the seas. Animals begin moving across the land. Each stage builds upon the one before it, suggesting that creation is not accidental or unstable but structured and purposeful.

The narrative repeatedly emphasizes that what God makes is good. This refrain is not filler. It establishes a foundation for how Genesis understands reality. The world is not presented as a trap, an illusion, or an accident. It is presented as a good gift created with intention. That starting point matters because it shapes how the book later describes brokenness. Genesis portrays evil not as the natural state of things, but as a distortion of something originally good.

Finally, humanity appears. Unlike the rest of creation, human beings are described as being made "in the image of God." The phrase carries deep significance. It suggests that human beings reflect something of the Creator's nature in ways that other forms of life do not. This image language points to dignity—human worth that exists before achievement—and it points to responsibility—humans as stewards who represent God's care within the created world.

Genesis places the first humans in a garden called Eden, a setting that represents harmony between humanity, nature, and God. Work exists within the garden, but it is meaningful and creative rather than exhausting. Relationships exist without shame or suspicion. The natural world provides abundance rather than resistance. In Eden, everything functions as it should because the relationships at the center of life are unbroken.

The world begins in order, and that order includes boundaries. Genesis does not portray boundaries as cruelty. It portrays them as part of what makes life stable and good. The garden is freedom with limits, and the limits are meant to protect life rather than restrict it.

The Fall: Freedom and Consequence

Within the garden stands a tree that represents the boundary of human freedom. Adam and Eve are permitted to enjoy every part of the garden except the fruit of this one tree. This command introduces a fundamental reality: freedom requires trust. The relationship between humanity and God depends not only on provision but also on obedience. The boundary serves as a reminder that humanity is not the ultimate authority over creation and that moral reality is not something humans invent.

A serpent enters the story and begins to question the command. Instead of directly denying God's instruction, the serpent raises doubt. It suggests that the boundary exists not for protection but for limitation, and it implies that God's motives are suspect. This is how temptation often works in Genesis. It rarely begins with open rebellion. It begins with suspicion. It begins by turning trust into doubt.

Adam and Eve face a decision. They can trust God's guidance, or they can act independently and define good and evil for themselves. Genesis frames the moment as more than a dietary mistake. It is a spiritual rupture. It is the choice to seek autonomy rather than relationship, self-rule rather than trust.

They choose independence.

The moment appears small at first—a single act of disobedience in the quiet setting of a garden. Yet the consequences are immediate and far-reaching. Shame enters the story as Adam and Eve become aware of vulnerability in a way they were not before. They attempt to hide from God, and when confronted, blame replaces trust. Adam blames Eve. Eve blames the serpent. The instinct to protect the self at the expense of relationship takes root immediately.

Genesis describes several consequences that will shape the rest of human history. Work becomes difficult, no longer experienced only as meaningful stewardship but as strain and resistance. Relationships become strained as power and conflict enter the human dynamic. The natural world begins to resist human effort, reflecting fracture beyond the human heart. Mortality becomes unavoidable, and the garden is lost. Humanity now carries both dignity and brokenness, which becomes one of Genesis's most enduring observations about the human condition.

The fall is not the end of the story, but it changes the environment in which every later story takes place. Genesis is showing readers the origin of fracture: fracture between humans and God, between humans and one another, and between humans and creation itself.

Cain and Abel: The First Violence

The next generation reveals how quickly corruption spreads. Adam and Eve's sons, Cain and Abel, both bring offerings to God. Abel's offering is accepted, while Cain's is not. The text does not fully explain why, but it focuses on Cain's response. Cain becomes angry, and his anger becomes a defining moment. Genesis treats anger as a crossroads. It can be addressed with humility, or it can be allowed to harden into resentment.

God confronts Cain before the anger turns into action. The warning is personal and direct. Cain is told that destructive choices are near and that he must master what is rising inside him. In other words, Cain is not treated as helpless. He is treated as responsible. He has agency. He can choose.

Cain ignores the warning.

He invites his brother into the field and kills him. The first murder in human history occurs within the first family, and Genesis makes the point unmistakable: violence is not introduced by strangers. It begins where trust should be strongest. The narrative demonstrates how jealousy, resentment, and wounded pride can escalate into irreversible decisions. Cain does not merely kill Abel. He attempts to eliminate the source of his perceived humiliation.

God confronts Cain about what he has done, and Cain responds with denial and deflection, asking the famous question, "Am I my brother's keeper?" The question echoes across history because it captures a timeless human impulse: the refusal to accept responsibility for others. Genesis answers that question not by argument but by consequence. Cain's act fractures his relationship to the ground itself. He becomes restless, alienated, and unstable.

Cain is judged and forced to leave his home, becoming a wanderer. Yet even within judgment there is mercy. God marks Cain for protection so that others will not take revenge against him. Genesis introduces a tension that will appear repeatedly throughout the book: justice and grace exist side by side. Judgment does not erase mercy, and mercy does not cancel accountability.

The Spread of Corruption

As generations pass, humanity multiplies across the earth. Cities form. Culture develops. People build, create, and organize. Genesis does not deny human creativity even in a fallen world. But the moral condition of society deteriorates, and the narrative portrays a growing momentum toward violence and corruption. The text summarizes the situation with stark clarity: every inclination of the human heart had become focused on evil.

This description is severe, and it is meant to be. Genesis is portraying a world where the internal fracture of the fall has expanded into a cultural norm. When corruption becomes normal, individuals no longer need to choose evil consciously. Evil becomes embedded in social habits, economic practices, and power structures.

In response, God chooses to intervene. Yet even in this moment of crisis, one individual stands apart from the corruption surrounding him. His name is Noah, and the text describes him as righteous within his generation. Genesis does not present Noah as perfect, but it does present him as different. He is a man who still responds to God in a world that no longer does.

The Flood: Judgment and Preservation

Noah is instructed to build an enormous vessel capable of preserving life through a coming flood. The task likely appeared absurd to those around him. Constructing a massive boat far from open water would have seemed irrational, even embarrassing. Yet Noah obeys. Genesis emphasizes obedience not as blind compliance but as trust expressed through action. Noah builds, prepares, and gathers what will be needed long before any visible evidence justifies the effort.

Eventually, the flood arrives. Rain falls for forty days while waters rise across the earth, covering the land and sweeping away the violent society that had dominated the world. The flood represents both judgment and cleansing. Corruption is confronted, but life is preserved. The same waters that destroy also reset, washing away what had become deeply toxic.

When the waters recede, Noah and his family emerge into a renewed world. God establishes a covenant with Noah, promising never again to destroy the earth by flood. A rainbow becomes the sign of this promise, serving as a visible reminder that judgment will not be the only divine response to human brokenness.

The world begins again, but Genesis is careful not to romanticize the restart. Noah's own failure after the flood reveals that the problem was never only external. Human nature has not been cured by catastrophe. The flood addresses corruption on a societal level, but it does not remove the deeper fracture within the human heart.

Babel: Humanity's Pride

After the flood, human communities spread and rebuild. Cities grow again. New societies emerge. People regain confidence in their ability to shape the future, and the desire for power returns quickly. A group settles in a region called Shinar and decides to construct a massive tower reaching toward heaven. The project represents human ambition and collective pride. The builders seek to establish significance, unity, and security through their own achievement.

They want control, but they also want certainty. They fear scattering, fear vulnerability, and fear dependence. Genesis portrays Babel not only as arrogance but as a human attempt to stabilize life apart from God. The tower becomes a symbol of humanity's desire to define destiny on its own terms.

In response, God intervenes by confusing language. Communication breaks down, cooperation collapses, and the people disperse across the earth. The city becomes known as

Babel, a name associated with confusion. The story reinforces a recurring theme throughout Genesis: pride eventually collapses because it cannot hold what it tries to control.

Babel closes the first major movement of Genesis. The problem is established on a universal scale. Humanity is fractured. Violence and pride have spread. Efforts to build security without God produce division rather than stability.

And then the narrative turns.

The Call of Abraham: A New Beginning

After Babel, Genesis shifts dramatically. Instead of following the story of the entire human race, the narrative narrows its focus to a single individual: Abraham. The shift is not random. Genesis has shown that humanity as a whole cannot repair the world. Now the story introduces a different strategy. God begins to work through one family as the seed of blessing that will eventually reach outward.

God calls Abraham to leave his homeland and travel to a new land that will be revealed later. Abraham must abandon familiar territory, extended family networks, religious norms, and economic security without knowing where the journey will lead. This call requires trust that cannot be proved in advance. It is faith expressed through movement.

God accompanies the command with a set of remarkable promises. Abraham will become the father of a great nation. His descendants will inherit a specific land. Through his family, all nations of the earth will ultimately be blessed. These promises form the foundation of the biblical covenant and become the driving force behind the rest of Genesis.

Abraham's journey is not without struggle. At times, he demonstrates deep faith. At other moments, he acts out of fear or impatience. He lies about his wife to protect himself. He attempts to force outcomes through human solutions when waiting feels impossible. Genesis does not hide these failures. It portrays faith as real trust mixed with real weakness.

Yet despite Abraham's uncertainty, the promise continues. Late in life, Abraham and his wife Sarah receive the son they had long hoped for. Isaac is born, and the covenant line moves forward through him. Genesis makes clear that the promise is not upheld by Abraham's perfection but by God's commitment.

Isaac and Jacob: A Complicated Family

Isaac grows into adulthood and becomes the father of twin sons, Esau and Jacob. Esau is strong, impulsive, and drawn to the outdoors. Jacob is thoughtful, strategic, and often calculating. From the beginning, tension develops between the brothers. Their rivalry is intensified by parental favoritism and by the importance of inheritance, blessing, and leadership within the family.

The conflict deepens when Jacob manipulates circumstances to obtain both his brother's birthright and his father's blessing. In the ancient world, these were not sentimental rituals. They were transfers of authority and future. Jacob's deception reshapes the family's direction, and it forces him to flee to survive Esau's rage.

For many years, Jacob lived away from home. During this time, he marries, raises children, and accumulates wealth, but his life is marked by struggle and consequence. Genesis portrays him as a man who tries to control outcomes and repeatedly discovers that control has a cost. He experiences deception from others in the same ways he once deceived, and the pattern becomes a painful form of correction.

The most mysterious moment occurs as Jacob prepares to return home and face the brother he wronged years earlier. One night, he wrestles with a mysterious figure until morning. The struggle leaves him wounded, but it also leaves him changed. He receives a new name: Israel. The name reflects a lifelong struggle with God and humanity, and it signals a turning point. Jacob's identity is no longer defined only by manipulation. It is defined by encounter, humility, and perseverance.

Jacob's twelve sons will eventually become the twelve tribes that form the nation of Israel. The promise continues through them, but Genesis also shows how fragile that promise can feel when family conflict intensifies.

Joseph: Betrayal and Redemption

The final major section of Genesis focuses on Joseph, one of Jacob's sons. Joseph's story begins with conflict inside the family. Jacob favors him openly, giving him a special coat that symbolizes preference over his brothers. Joseph also shares dreams suggesting that his family will one day bow before him. Whether Joseph intends arrogance or simply naivety, the effect is the same. Resentment grows quickly, fed by favoritism and wounded pride.

Eventually, Joseph's brothers seize an opportunity to act. They throw him into a pit and sell him to traders traveling to Egypt. To conceal their actions, they deceive their father into believing Joseph has been killed. Joseph disappears from the family, and the household is fractured by grief and secrecy.

In Egypt, Joseph is sold into the household of a government official. Through diligence and integrity, he earns responsibility, but adversity returns when he is falsely accused and thrown into prison. Genesis does not gloss over the injustice. It portrays Joseph as a man who suffers not because of direct wrongdoing but because of the brokenness of the world around him.

Even in prison, Joseph's character stands out. He interprets dreams for fellow prisoners, and his reputation eventually reaches Pharaoh. Pharaoh summons him to interpret troubling dreams about a coming famine. Joseph explains that years of abundance will be followed by years of severe scarcity, and he offers practical wisdom for preparation. Pharaoh recognizes his ability and appoints him to oversee the nation's planning.

Joseph rises from prisoner to national leader, a reversal that displays one of Genesis's key themes: providence. What others intended for harm becomes part of a larger purpose that Joseph could not have imagined at the time.

When famine strikes, people from surrounding regions come to Egypt seeking food, including Joseph's own brothers. They do not recognize him, but Joseph recognizes them. The moment carries weight because Joseph now holds power over the people who once stripped him of everything. Genesis slows down here because this is where the story's moral and emotional resolution takes place.

Joseph tests his brothers, not to torment them, but to see whether they have changed. He eventually reveals his identity and chooses forgiveness. His words capture one of the central themes of Genesis: "What you meant for evil, God meant for good." This is not a denial of evil. It is a statement about the possibility of redemption even when evil has been done.

Joseph brings his family to Egypt, preserving them through the famine and keeping the covenant line alive. Genesis ends not with a complete resolution of the human problem, but with a clear preservation of the promise. A family is saved. Reconciliation occurs. The future remains open, but the direction of the story is established.

The narrative that began with creation now ends with a family preserved through forgiveness and providence.

And the promise is still unfolding.

Chapter 5

Key Themes of Genesis

I will bless those who bless you, and whoever curses you, I will curse; and all peoples on earth will be blessed through you.
—Genesis 12:3

The events recorded in Genesis span centuries and involves many individuals living in different circumstances and cultures. The book moves from the origin of the world to the development of a single family, and along the way, it introduces scenes that feel very different from one another: a garden, a flood, desert journeys, rival siblings, and political power in Egypt. Yet beneath the variety of stories, several central ideas appear repeatedly throughout the narrative. These themes provide a framework for understanding both the human condition and the unfolding relationship between God and humanity.

Genesis is not simply a collection of ancient stories. It is a book built around patterns—moral patterns, relational patterns, and spiritual patterns. Certain truths surface again and again as the narrative moves from creation to the lives of Abraham's descendants. Those truths connect the experiences of the characters to larger questions about identity, morality, faith, and purpose.

When readers grasp these themes, the stories begin to fit together. The narrative gains coherence. Events that might otherwise seem disconnected start to form a unified picture. Genesis becomes less like a chain of isolated episodes and more like a single story told across generations: a story explaining what went wrong, why it persists, and how God begins to move history toward restoration.

The book keeps returning to the same realities.

Creation and fracture.

Blessing and rebellion.

Promise and delay.

Failure and mercy.

That repetition is not accidental. It is how Genesis teaches. It shows the reader the same truth from multiple angles until the pattern becomes impossible to miss.

Creation and Human Dignity

Genesis begins with a declaration that reshapes how humanity understands itself.

Human beings are created intentionally.

The opening chapter describes the formation of the world in careful stages, culminating in the creation of humanity. Unlike the animals, which are described as emerging from the earth, human beings are said to be made in the image of God. This phrase carries profound significance. It suggests that humans reflect something of the Creator's nature in ways that other forms of life do not. Humanity occupies a unique position within the created order—neither divine nor merely animal, but capable of moral responsibility, creativity, and relationship.

The theme of the image of God establishes that human life carries inherent value. This idea stands in contrast to many ancient societies in which status determined worth. In much of the ancient world, rulers and elites were often viewed as possessing higher dignity than ordinary people. Slaves, foreigners, and the poor could be treated as expendable because their value was defined socially rather than intrinsically.

Genesis offers a different perspective. Every person shares the same fundamental dignity. Worth is not determined by power, wealth, intelligence, productivity, or social position. It arises from the reality that every human being reflects something of the

Creator. Genesis begins by placing value at the core of human identity before describing any human achievement.

That matters because human beings often reverse the order.

People tend to assume that worth must be proven. They build identities around performance, usefulness, recognition, or control. Genesis cuts against that instinct. It says value comes first. Life is sacred before success, before influence, before accomplishment. The text does not present dignity as something to be earned after proving oneself. It presents dignity as something received at the beginning.

This theme shapes the entire biblical narrative. Human dignity does not come from accomplishment. It comes from creation. In modern terms, Genesis presents identity as something received, not something earned. It challenges any system—ancient or modern—that ranks human value by performance, usefulness, or status.

Alongside dignity comes responsibility. Adam and Eve are placed in the garden not merely to enjoy its beauty but to care for it. They are entrusted with stewardship over the natural world, tasked with cultivating and protecting what has been given to them. This portrayal suggests that humans are not owners of creation. They are caretakers, responsible for tending rather than exploiting.

Genesis also emphasizes that human life is relational. Adam and Eve are depicted interacting directly with God through communication, guidance, and accountability. The text presents the relationship with God not as a later religious concept but as part of the original human design. Humanity is created for relationship—with one another, with creation, and with the Creator.

This means that isolation is not the original pattern.

Neither is domination.

Neither is alienation.

Genesis begins with connection, purpose, and entrusted responsibility. That starting point is essential because it clarifies that brokenness is not normal in the deepest sense. It may be familiar, but it is not original.

Freedom and Responsibility

Genesis also emphasizes that human dignity includes freedom.

Adam and Eve are given broad permission within the garden. They may enjoy its abundance, cultivate its resources, and explore its beauty. Only one boundary exists: they are not to eat from the tree of the knowledge of good and evil. The command is simple, yet its implications are profound because it introduces a moral reality into human life.

The boundary represents a test of trust rather than a restrictive rule. It reminds humanity that freedom exists within a larger moral framework. Genesis portrays freedom not as the absence of limits, but as the ability to live meaningfully within wise limits. The boundary in Eden functions like a line that protects life rather than reduces it, and it invites humanity to trust God's definition of good.

Freedom always carries responsibility.

This is one of Genesis's clearest claims about human life. Choice is a gift, but it is never weightless. Decisions do not remain private, isolated, or harmless simply because they are personal. Choices shape relationships. They alter futures. They create trajectories.

When Adam and Eve choose to eat the forbidden fruit, the narrative demonstrates how the misuse of freedom can disrupt relationships and alter the course of history. The decision introduces shame, mistrust, and separation into the human experience. It also reveals how quickly freedom can become self-justification. Rather than owning their choice, Adam and Eve move toward blame, and the pattern of relational fracture begins.

Genesis repeatedly shows that choices have weight. The consequences extend far beyond the original moment. Sin is not portrayed as merely an internal feeling or a private issue. It creates ripples outward, shaping families, communities, and futures.

This pattern continues throughout the rest of Genesis. Cain chooses violence instead of reconciliation. Jacob chooses deception instead of honesty. Joseph's brothers choose betrayal instead of loyalty. Each decision produces consequences that ripple through families and communities, and those ripples often extend for decades. Actions rarely remain isolated. They create patterns that others inherit.

This is one reason Genesis feels so realistic.

The book understands that one act often becomes a pattern, and a pattern often becomes a legacy. One generation's fear, pride, or dishonesty can become the next generation's burden. In the same way, one generation's courage, integrity, or repentance can become the next generation's blessing.

Genesis does not portray human beings as passive victims of fate. It presents individuals as active participants whose choices matter. This view carries both dignity and accountability. Humans are not robots, but they are also not excused from the consequences of their decisions.

Human Rebellion and the Spread of Sin

After the fall in Eden, Genesis traces the rapid spread of corruption through human society.

The first family already reflects the tension between dignity and brokenness. Cain's jealousy leads him to murder his brother Abel, introducing violence into the human story almost immediately. Genesis portrays this as more than a tragic event. It is a revelation of what happens when resentment is allowed to grow unchecked and when pride refuses correction.

The consequences escalate quickly. Within a few generations, violence becomes widespread. The narrative describing the era of Noah portrays a world dominated by moral chaos. Human behavior has become so destructive that the text describes every inclination of the human heart as bent toward evil. The situation is severe, and Genesis presents it as a culture-wide collapse rather than isolated incidents.

That escalation matters.

Genesis is showing that sin spreads. It does not remain contained within one act, one person, or one household. It distorts desires, then relationships, then systems. The corruption that begins in Eden becomes visible in a family, then in a culture, then across the earth.

The flood story represents a dramatic response to this corruption. The narrative portrays the flood as both judgment and cleansing, confronting the destructive patterns that had overtaken humanity. Yet Genesis does not present the flood as a permanent cure. Even after the waters recede and the world begins again, the deeper problem remains unresolved.

Human nature has not fundamentally changed.

The builders of Babel illustrate this reality. Instead of dispersing across the earth, they attempt to consolidate power and secure identity through a tower that symbolizes collective greatness. They seek recognition, control, and security built by human effort alone. The project reflects a recurring pattern throughout Genesis: humanity's desire to define good and evil independently, to establish significance apart from God, and to create stability through pride rather than trust.

Sin spreads, but Genesis is careful to show that corruption never fully eliminates the possibility of redemption. Even in the moments of greatest failure, mercy appears. Even when judgment comes, it does not end the story. Genesis presents rebellion as real and devastating, but it also presents God as persistent rather than absent.

That balance is important.

Genesis does not minimize evil, but it does not surrender to it either.

Covenant and Divine Promise

One of the most significant turning points in Genesis occurs when God calls Abraham.

After tracing the struggles of humanity as a whole, the narrative shifts to focus on one individual and one family. This shift signals a change in how restoration will unfold. Rather than transforming the entire world in one sweeping act, God begins working through a specific lineage, establishing a covenant relationship that will become the foundation for the rest of Scripture.

The covenant with Abraham introduces a new direction in the story. God makes several promises: Abraham will become the father of a great nation; his descendants will inherit a particular land; and through his family, all nations of the earth will ultimately be blessed.

These promises are central not only to Genesis but to the entire biblical narrative. They provide continuity across generations and offer a forward trajectory for the story. They also introduce a crucial theme: God's plan moves through history in a way that often looks slow, fragile, and uncertain.

The promise unfolds gradually.

That is one of the hardest things for modern readers to accept. Genesis does not present restoration as instant. It unfolds through generations, setbacks, detours, and waiting. Abraham receives the promise, but he does not see its full outcome. The covenant stretches beyond his lifetime.

The covenant is remarkable because it does not depend on Abraham's perfection. Genesis shows Abraham struggling with fear, doubt, and impatience. At times, he attempts to protect himself through deception. At other times, he tries to force outcomes through strategy rather than trust. He is not presented as a flawless model of faith.

Yet the covenant continues.

Its stability does not depend on Abraham's consistency. It depends on God's commitment. This theme continues through Isaac, Jacob, and Joseph. Each generation experiences weakness and failure, yet the promise remains intact. Even when the family line is threatened by famine, conflict, or betrayal, the covenant does not disappear.

Genesis reveals a God who remains faithful even when people do not. The covenant persists because the promise is carried by divine persistence rather than human perfection.

That theme offers one of the book's deepest forms of hope. If the future of redemption depended entirely on human steadiness, the story would collapse quickly. But Genesis says the future is carried by something stronger than human consistency.

Family Conflict and Human Imperfection

Another striking feature of Genesis is its honest portrayal of family relationships.

Many of the central conflicts occur within families rather than between distant enemies. Genesis repeatedly reveals how jealousy, favoritism, and competition can fracture even the closest relationships. The book does not idealize family as a safe refuge. It portrays family as one of the primary places where both love and brokenness are most exposed.

Cain kills Abel. Jacob deceives his father and steals Esau's blessing. Joseph's brothers sell him into slavery. These stories demonstrate how deeply human weakness can affect family life. Favoritism creates resentment. Pride fuels rivalry. Insecurity drives manipulation. Fear justifies betrayal.

The Bible does not attempt to hide these failures. It records them openly, and this honesty gives Genesis an unusual realism. The characters are not polished heroes who always act wisely. They struggle with the same motivations modern readers recognize: the desire to be seen, the fear of being replaced, the craving for approval, the impulse to protect oneself at all costs.

The families in Genesis feel real because they are complicated.

That complexity is part of the book's power. It does not present dysfunction as abnormal or shocking. It presents it as painfully familiar. And yet it refuses to treat fracture as the end of the story.

The stories also reveal that broken relationships do not always remain broken forever. Jacob eventually returns to reconcile with Esau. Joseph forgives the brothers who betrayed him. These resolutions are not simplistic. They involve time, humility, fear, and often deep emotional cost, but they point toward a central theme: relationships that have been fractured can still move toward restoration.

Genesis suggests that family conflict is not new, but neither is forgiveness. In the same way that dysfunction can be passed down, reconciliation can also reshape the future.

That is one of the book's quiet strengths.

It tells the truth about family pain without surrendering to cynicism.

Divine Providence

The final chapters of Genesis emphasize the theme of providence—the idea that God works through events, including painful ones, to accomplish larger purposes.

Joseph's story provides the clearest illustration. His brothers intend harm when they sell him into slavery. Later, false accusations led to imprisonment. At multiple points, Joseph's life appears to be defined by injustice and misfortune, and nothing in his circumstances suggests a clear path toward redemption.

Yet these events ultimately place him in a position where he can interpret Pharaoh's dreams and prepare Egypt for famine. What appears to be a series of disasters becomes a pathway toward preservation. Joseph rises from slavery to leadership, and through his planning, entire populations survive. Even the family that betrayed him is preserved.

Joseph recognizes this pattern when he tells his brothers, "You meant evil against me, but God meant it for good." The statement captures the essence of providence. It does not deny the evil that occurred. It does not excuse betrayal. It simply acknowledges that human intentions, while flawed and destructive, do not have ultimate authority over the outcome of the story.

Human intentions may be corrupted.
Divine purposes continue moving forward.

Providence becomes one of Genesis's strongest answers to the question of brokenness. The book does not claim that suffering is good, but it does claim that suffering is not always final. God can work through tragedy without being the author of cruelty, and restoration can emerge through paths that look like loss.

That does not remove pain.

It gives pain context.

Joseph's story does not say everything happens for a shallow or sentimental reason. It says God is not defeated by what human beings do. Even betrayal, injustice, and delay can become part of a larger movement toward preservation.

Redemption and Hope

Despite the many failures described throughout Genesis, the book never abandons hope.

Each generation struggles with the same patterns of pride, fear, and ambition. Yet each generation also encounters moments of grace and restoration. Noah survives the flood. Abraham receives a son despite advanced age. Jacob returns home after years of exile. Joseph forgives the brothers who betrayed him.

These moments reveal that redemption does not emerge from human perfection. It emerges from patience, from forgiveness, and from the persistence of divine promise. Genesis portrays God as continuing to engage humanity even when humanity repeatedly fails. The story moves forward not because people finally become flawless but because grace continues to appear.

This is one of the most important truths in the book.

Genesis does not build hope on human improvement alone. It builds hope on divine faithfulness.

Genesis closes with Jacob's family living in Egypt, preserved from famine through Joseph's leadership. The future remains uncertain, and the covenant promises have not yet been fully realized. Yet the story ends with survival, reconciliation, and the continuation of the promise.

The book finishes where the larger biblical story truly begins: with a people carrying both human weakness and divine hope.

The promise still stands, and the unfolding story of redemption continues beyond Genesis.

Chapter 6

Where People Often Get It Wrong

*Now the serpent was more crafty than any of the wild animals
the Lord God had made. He said to the woman, "Did God really
say, 'You must not eat from any tree in the garden'?"*
—Genesis 3:1

Genesis is one of the most widely discussed and frequently misunderstood books in the Bible. Because it addresses foundational questions about origins, identity, and human nature, readers often approach the text with strong assumptions already in place. Those assumptions shape interpretation long before the reader has a chance to hear the book on its own terms.

Some misunderstandings arise from modern cultural debates that pressure Genesis to answer questions it was not written to answer. Others emerge when readers focus on isolated passages without seeing the broader narrative structure. In many cases, confusion develops simply because readers approach an ancient text using modern expectations—expectations shaped by scientific categories, Western individualism, and a highly literal "instruction manual" approach to meaning.

Clarifying these issues helps readers engage Genesis more thoughtfully. It also helps them hear what the text is actually trying to say. Genesis speaks into some of the deepest questions people ask about life, purpose, morality, and meaning. When the book is misunderstood, those questions can become clouded by arguments that distract from its central message.

Understanding what Genesis is—and what it is not—allows readers to approach the text with greater clarity, humility, and realism. Genesis is not fragile. It does not need to be propped up with forced readings. But it does need to be read with the right posture: as ancient Scripture that addresses timeless human realities.

Most of the confusion comes from one mistake.

People demand that Genesis be what they want it to be, instead of letting it be what it is.

Genesis is narrative theology. It is a story that teaches truth. It is not a modern textbook, not a lab report, not a political manifesto, and not a motivational poster. It's bigger than those categories, and it refuses to be reduced.

When readers force Genesis into the wrong framework, they don't just misread a few verses. They miss the entire point.

Misunderstanding 1: Genesis Is Primarily a Scientific Explanation

One of the most common debates surrounding Genesis centers on the mechanics of creation. For many modern readers, the opening chapters raise immediate questions about science, time, and the structure of the universe.

How long were the days of creation?
How does Genesis relate to modern scientific theories about the origin of the universe?
Is the narrative describing literal events or symbolic language?

These questions have generated centuries of discussion. Scholars, theologians, and scientists have proposed a wide range of interpretations in attempts to understand how Genesis relates to modern discoveries. The questions are not insignificant, and they deserve careful thought.

But they are often misplaced.

Genesis was written in a world very different from the modern scientific age. Ancient audiences were not asking questions about astrophysics, cosmology, genetics, or evolutionary biology. Those categories did not exist, and the text is not framed as a technical explanation using modern scientific vocabulary.

Instead, people in the ancient Near East were asking different questions entirely.

Who created the world?

Why does the universe exist?

What kind of God rules reality?

What is the role of human beings within creation?

The opening chapter of Genesis answers those questions with remarkable clarity. The universe is not the result of chaotic forces or rival deities battling for dominance. It is the result of intentional design by a single Creator. The focus is theological, not technical. Genesis is less concerned with explaining the physical mechanisms of creation than with establishing meaning: that creation is purposeful, ordered, and accountable to a Creator who stands above it.

This is not a dodge. It is a category issue.

Genesis is not trying to tell you *how* God created in the same way a scientific journal explains process. Genesis is telling you *who* created, *why* creation exists, and *what kind of world* this is. A world with purpose. A world with order. A world where moral reality is real, not invented.

When readers reduce the opening chapters to a scientific debate, they often miss the deeper claims being made. Genesis is addressing purpose, not lab procedure. It is addressing identity, not measurement. It is explaining why the world exists, why human life carries significance, and why moral reality is not something people invent as they go.

In other words, Genesis is not trying to compete with science. It is doing something different. It is announcing who God is, what creation is, and who humans are in relation to both.

A lot of modern arguments miss this because they assume Genesis must either be a modern scientific account or it must be meaningless. That's a false choice. Genesis is not written to answer every modern question, but it answers the ancient ones with force.

And those ancient questions still sit underneath modern life.

Misunderstanding 2: The Characters Are Moral Heroes

Another common misunderstanding involves the people who appear throughout Genesis. Some readers assume these individuals are meant to serve primarily as moral examples—models of ideal faith or perfect behavior. Because Abraham, Isaac, Jacob, and Joseph become central figures in the unfolding covenant, it is easy to assume the book is presenting them as polished heroes.

Yet a closer reading reveals something very different.

The characters in Genesis are deeply flawed.

Abraham lies about his wife to protect himself when he fears foreign rulers. He compromises integrity in moments of anxiety and attempts to manipulate outcomes rather than trusting God patiently. Jacob deceives his father, exploits his brother's weakness, and uses strategy to seize what was not his to take. Joseph, though later portrayed as wise and forgiving, initially displays immaturity and arrogance that fuels resentment in his family. Even the most sympathetic figures are not immune to fear, self-protection, or shortsightedness.

Genesis does not hide these failures. It records them openly.

This honesty is striking. Many ancient stories exaggerate the virtues of their central figures while minimizing their weaknesses. Genesis often does the opposite. It shows the complexity of human nature. The people in these stories wrestle with fear, insecurity, ambition, jealousy, and doubt—the same forces that shape human behavior today.

They are not idealized heroes. They are recognizably human.

The purpose of Genesis is not to provide a collection of perfect role models. Instead, the narrative demonstrates how divine purposes continue moving forward even through imperfect people. Human weakness does not stop the story. The covenant continues anyway. Genesis is less interested in showcasing human greatness than in highlighting divine faithfulness.

That matters because if you misread the characters, you misread the message.

If you expect heroes, their failures will either disappoint you into cynicism or push you into denial. Some readers sanitize these stories to protect their view of "faith people." Others reject the Bible entirely because the characters look too human.

But Genesis is realistic about people on purpose.

It shows you what God works with. It shows you what God repairs. It shows you that faith is not clean and linear. It's often messy, slow, and shaped through failure and mercy.

Misunderstanding 3: The Early Chapters Are Isolated Stories

Another misunderstanding arises when readers treat the early chapters of Genesis as a series of unrelated stories.

Creation.

The fall.

Cain and Abel.

The flood.

The tower of Babel.

Many people first encounter these narratives individually during childhood or religious education, often presented as separate moral lessons: "Don't lie," "Don't disobey," "Don't be jealous." While those lessons may be present, Genesis is doing more than moral instruction. It is building a sequence.

Each story builds upon the one before it.

Creation establishes the goodness of the world and the dignity of humanity. The fall introduces rebellion and a broken relationship. Cain and Abel show how quickly internal fracture becomes external violence, even within the first family. The flood reveals how corruption can expand until it dominates entire societies, creating cultures where violence becomes normal. Babel shows humanity attempting to assert control and unity apart from God, building identity through pride and self-determination.

This progression reveals something important about human nature.

The problem is not isolated. It spreads.

What begins as a single act of mistrust in a garden expands into societal violence and cultural arrogance. The early chapters function as a diagnosis of the human condition. They explain why the world contains both beauty and chaos and why human history often moves in cycles of ambition, conflict, and collapse.

Genesis is not a scrapbook. It's a narrative arc.

And that arc has a purpose. It brings you to a turning point.

Most importantly, these chapters prepare the reader for the call of Abraham. After tracing the failure of humanity as a whole, Genesis narrows its focus to a single family. That narrowing is not random. It is a strategy.

Restoration will begin there.

When readers treat the early chapters as disconnected stories, they miss the movement Genesis is building: a widening fracture that requires a focused covenant response. Genesis is showing you that humanity cannot fix itself from the inside. So, God initiates a promise through a family that will eventually bless the nations.

Misunderstanding 4: Genesis Is Only About Ancient History

Because Genesis describes events from the distant past, some readers assume the book has little relevance to modern life. The cultural setting appears remote—shepherds traveling through deserts, family disputes inside tribal networks, ancient customs, and unfamiliar geography. At first glance, the world of Genesis seems far removed from contemporary experience.

The technology is different.

The societies are different.

The geography is unfamiliar.

Yet beneath those cultural differences, the core struggles described in Genesis remain remarkably familiar. Families still experience rivalry and favoritism. Individuals still wrestle with ambition, fear, insecurity, and moral compromise. Communities still struggle with pride, power, and the desire for control.

The circumstances have changed, but human nature has not.

Genesis captures patterns of behavior that appear in every generation. Jealousy still destroys relationships. Fear still drives dishonesty. Ambition still tempts individuals to pursue success at the cost of integrity. Leaders still face moments where they must decide whether they will use power to serve or to protect themselves. Families still carry generational wounds that echo for decades.

For this reason, Genesis often functions less like a history book and more like a mirror. Readers recognize themselves within its stories. The people in Genesis live in an ancient world, but the emotional and moral tensions remain familiar: the desire to belong, the fear of being replaced, the temptation to manipulate outcomes, and the longing for blessing without surrender.

Genesis speaks across centuries because it addresses realities every generation encounters.

If someone reads Genesis and says, "That has nothing to do with me," it usually means they have not read it closely, or they have protected themselves from what it reveals. Genesis is not just describing an ancient world. It's describing the human heart.

Misunderstanding 5: The Book Ends Without Resolution

Some readers finish Genesis with a sense that the story is incomplete. The book ends with Joseph forgiving his brothers and the family settling in Egypt. The immediate conflict is resolved, yet the broader problems introduced earlier—sin, suffering, and separation from God—remain.

That tension is real, and Genesis does not hide it.

But the ending is not accidental.

Genesis was never intended to function as a self-contained narrative. It is the opening movement of a much larger story that continues through the rest of the Bible. Its purpose is not to tie every thread in a neat bow. Its purpose is to establish the problem and launch the promise.

By the end of Genesis, the covenant established with Abraham remains active. His descendants have grown into a large family, but they have not yet become the nation that was promised. They live in a foreign land, dependent on the protection of a powerful empire. They are safe for now, but they are not home. They have survived, but they are not yet free.

The promise has begun, but it has not been fulfilled.

Genesis leaves readers at the start of a long journey. The descendants of Jacob will grow into a nation within Egypt. Over time, they will become enslaved. Their story will continue in Exodus as God raises up Moses to lead them toward freedom.

Genesis introduces the problem.
Genesis introduces the promise.
The resolution unfolds across the rest of Scripture.

The brokenness of humanity is clear, and so is the possibility of restoration. Genesis ends not with a final resolution, but with direction. The trajectory is set. The story has only just begun.

And that is part of Genesis's honesty.

It refuses to pretend the world is fixed in a single chapter. It shows the fracture. It introduces the promise. Then it hands you off to the next movement of the story—because restoration is not a slogan. It's a mission.

Chapter 7

What It Means for Modern Life

*So God created mankind in his own image, in the image of God he
created them; male and female he created them.*
—*Genesis 1:27*

Genesis describes events that took place thousands of years ago in
a world very different from our own. The cultures, technologies,
and political structures described in the book belong to a distant
era. Shepherds move across deserts with their flocks. Families live
in tents rather than cities. Communication travels slowly, and
survival often depends on seasonal patterns of rain and harvest.
On the surface, the world of Genesis can feel remote from the
modern reader, shaped by customs and assumptions that no
longer define daily life.

But distance in time does not mean distance in relevance.

Under the ancient details lies the same battlefield every
generation walks through: identity, ambition, fear, trust,
compromise, family fracture, and the stubborn hope that life can
still be repaired. Genesis matters because it refuses to
sentimentalize the human condition. It names what is true about
people and then shows what God does in the middle of it.

The circumstances change, but human nature does not
change as quickly.

This is one of the reasons Genesis remains significant. It
allows readers to see enduring patterns clearly, without the noise.
The people in Genesis don't have modern tools, but they carry
modern pressures in human form. They still want security. They
still want control. They still want blessings without surrender.
They still fear being exposed, replaced, or forgotten. Genesis gives

those realities a storyline and, by doing so, helps readers better understand themselves.

The book is ancient, but the pressures it describes are not. People still wrestle with worth, power, rivalry, responsibility, compromise, and hope. Genesis doesn't just offer advice. It offers diagnosis and direction. It shows what breaks people, what breaks families, and what it takes—over time—for anything to move toward restoration.

Identity: Worth Beyond Achievement

One of the most significant ideas introduced in Genesis is the concept that human beings are created in the image of God. This idea appears in the opening chapter of the book and establishes a foundation for understanding human identity that remains deeply relevant in the modern world.

Human life is intentional. Human life carries dignity.

In many ancient societies, a person's worth depended largely on social status. Kings, nobles, and wealthy individuals were often considered superior to ordinary people. Those with power determined the value of others, and individuals without status frequently lived with little protection or recognition. Human worth could be assigned, withheld, or manipulated depending on rank and circumstance.

Genesis presents a radically different perspective.

Every human being reflects the Creator.

This truth places every person on equal ground at the deepest level. Dignity does not depend on intelligence, strength, wealth, appearance, productivity, or social influence. Instead, dignity emerges from the reality that every human life has been created with purpose. A person's value is not something earned after achievement. It is present from the beginning.

That one idea cuts through modern pressure like a blade.

Today, identity is often built on performance. Careers, accomplishments, financial success, educational status, and public recognition become the measures by which individuals evaluate themselves and others. People are trained—sometimes openly, often subtly—to prove their worth through output. Even rest becomes something you feel guilty for if it doesn't "produce."

But these markers of identity are unstable.

Careers change. Wealth fluctuates. Recognition fades. Platforms disappear. Success that once seemed secure can vanish through failure, illness, recession, rejection, betrayal, or age. When identity depends entirely on external success, it becomes fragile. A person may feel strong in seasons of achievement and hollow in seasons of loss. And when the scoreboard becomes the source of worth, the fear of losing becomes a daily companion.

Genesis offers a deeper foundation.

Human worth begins before achievement. It begins with creation.

Understanding this principle reshapes how people see themselves and others. It encourages humility during success because success is no longer the source of ultimate worth. It preserves dignity during hardship because value is not erased when outcomes change. It also challenges the modern instinct to rank people by usefulness. Genesis declares that worth is not awarded by society and cannot be revoked by circumstances.

Identity grounded in creation cannot easily be taken away.

Leadership and Responsibility

Genesis also provides insight into the nature of leadership. From the earliest chapters, human beings are entrusted with responsibility for the world around them. Adam and Eve are placed in the garden with the task of cultivating and caring for creation. Their role is not merely to enjoy the environment but to steward it.

Responsibility appears before authority.

That order matters. Leadership in Genesis is not defined primarily by power, control, or status. It begins with the ability to care for what has been entrusted to you. Before anyone rules, someone must learn how to tend, protect, and act faithfully within limits. Leadership begins with stewardship—learning to handle what's in your hands before you demand what's in someone else's.

Joseph's story illustrates this principle with particular clarity. Early in life, Joseph experiences betrayal, injustice, and hardship. His brothers sell him into slavery, stripping him of security, family, and freedom. Later, after proving himself useful and trustworthy, he is falsely accused and imprisoned. At each stage of his journey, Joseph is placed in circumstances that could easily produce bitterness, passivity, or revenge.

Yet during these difficult years, Joseph develops qualities that eventually define his leadership. He works with diligence. He demonstrates wisdom. He maintains integrity even when circumstances seem unfair and even when no immediate reward appears likely. He learns how to act responsibly before he is given large-scale authority. He learns how to lead from the bottom, which is where most people either quit or compromise.

Those years weren't wasted. They were training.

When Joseph eventually rises to authority in Egypt, he does not treat leadership as an opportunity for personal power or vindication. Instead, he uses his position to prepare the nation for an approaching famine. He interprets risk accurately, plans ahead, and makes decisions that preserve life rather than inflate ego. He doesn't just react. He anticipates. He doesn't just survive. He builds resilience into the system.

His leadership saves countless lives.

The narrative demonstrates an important principle: leadership is often formed long before positions of authority appear. Character developed during adversity becomes the foundation for future influence. The experiences that feel like setbacks often shape the judgment necessary for responsible leadership later.

Modern life shows the same pattern. Leadership is not just titles, promotions, or visibility. It is the ability to act with integrity, foresight, and responsibility even when no one is applauding. Many people want authority before they have learned stewardship. Genesis reverses that order and warns—quietly but clearly—what happens when power is given to someone who has not been shaped by responsibility.

Authority without character rarely lasts. Character without authority eventually becomes influence.

Family Conflict and Reconciliation

Genesis presents families with striking honesty. Many of the most dramatic moments in the book occur not between nations but within households. Brothers compete for approval. Parents show favoritism. Misunderstandings deepen into resentment. Fear and insecurity distort relationships that should have been sources of trust.

These tensions create consequences that shape entire generations.

Cain murders Abel. Jacob deceives his father and steals Esau's blessing. Joseph's brothers sell him into slavery because of jealousy and resentment. These stories reveal how easily relationships can fracture when pride, insecurity, and favoritism take root. Genesis does not romanticize family life. It does not pretend that shared blood automatically produces health, honesty, or safety.

Family conflict remains just as familiar today.

Siblings still compete for recognition and approval. Parents still struggle to treat children equally. Old wounds still echo for decades, shaping how people react, avoid, accuse, or withdraw.

Families can be places of refuge, but they can also become the training ground for fear, comparison, and silent bitterness.

Genesis does not ignore these tensions. It acknowledges them directly, often with uncomfortable clarity. But the book also shows that conflict does not have to define the future forever. Moments of reconciliation appear throughout the narrative, reminding readers that broken relationships can sometimes be restored even after years of damage.

Jacob eventually confronts Esau after years of separation and fear. Joseph chooses forgiveness rather than revenge when his brothers come seeking food during the famine. Those reconciliations are not cheap. They cost pride. They cost control. They require risk. Genesis never pretends that forgiveness is the same thing as pretending nothing happened. It does not erase the past. It changes the trajectory.

Modern families face similar crossroads. Conflict can deepen divisions, or it can become the beginning of healing when individuals acknowledge both failure and forgiveness. Not every reconciliation looks the same. Not every relationship can return to what it was. Sometimes boundaries are necessary. Sometimes trust must be rebuilt slowly. But Genesis insists that brokenness does not always get the final word.

Restoration rarely happens quickly. But it remains possible.

Integrity Under Pressure

Another recurring theme in Genesis involves the testing of personal integrity. Joseph's life again provides one of the clearest examples. After being sold into slavery, he finds himself working within the household of an Egyptian official. Through diligence and competence, he gradually earns trust and responsibility. He performs well even in circumstances he did not choose and cannot control.

Then a new challenge appears.

Joseph is falsely accused of misconduct and imprisoned. The accusation destroys the stability he had built and places him in a situation where bitterness, dishonesty, or self-protective compromise would be understandable. He has every reason to become cynical. He has every reason to say, "This world rewards the wrong thing, so I'll do what I need to do."

Yet Joseph continues to act with integrity.

Even in prison, he earns the trust of those around him and demonstrates wisdom in interpreting dreams. These choices eventually led to his release and his rise to leadership within Egypt. The integrity he showed when no one was rewarding him becomes part of what makes him trustworthy when greater responsibility finally arrives.

Integrity is revealed most clearly under pressure.

Modern life presents the same tests, just dressed differently. Shortcuts look efficient. Silence looks safe. A little dishonesty looks harmless. Compromise gets explained as "strategy." People tell themselves they'll make it right later. Genesis refuses that logic. It shows that the decisions made in hidden places shape who you become in public places.

Genesis reminds readers that integrity shapes long-term outcomes. The decisions made when no one is watching often determine the kind of leader a person becomes when everyone is watching. Character is rarely formed in the spotlight. It is formed in private moments where a person chooses whether to remain truthful, faithful, and responsible when doing so costs something.

Integrity rarely produces instant reward. But it creates lasting influence.

Trust in Uncertain Futures

Another challenge that appears repeatedly in Genesis involves learning to trust when the future is unclear. Abraham's journey illustrates this reality vividly. When God calls him to leave his homeland, Abraham does not receive a detailed map of the destination. Instead, he is asked to begin traveling with the promise that the path will unfold over time.

The command requires faith.

Abraham must leave behind familiarity and security while trusting that the promises he has received will eventually come true. He is not given total clarity before movement begins. He is asked to step forward while much remains unknown. That is hard, because most people want certainty before obedience. They want the full picture before they risk a step.

Many people encounter similar moments in their own lives. Career transitions, major life decisions, family shifts, unexpected illness, financial instability, and personal loss can create seasons where the future feels uncertain, and the path forward is difficult to see. Modern life often rewards planning and control, so uncertainty can feel like failure rather than reality.

Genesis suggests something different.

Meaningful journeys often begin without complete clarity. Abraham does not fully understand the outcome of his journey when he begins it. The promise unfolds gradually across years and even generations. That means faith, in the Genesis sense, is not blind optimism or emotional denial. It is movement in the presence of uncertainty because trust is placed in something greater than immediate visibility.

This challenges the modern demand for guarantees. Many people delay action because they want certainty before responsibility, security before obedience, proof before trust. Genesis presents growth in a different way. It suggests that significant transformation often occurs when the destination is not yet visible, and the only thing you can do is take the next right step with what you know.

Faith is not the absence of questions. It is movement in the presence of them.

The Possibility of Redemption

Perhaps the most powerful message of Genesis is the possibility of redemption. Nearly every major character in the book experiences failure at some point in the narrative. Fear, deception, jealousy, betrayal, compromise, and grief appear repeatedly across generations.

Abraham struggles with fear and doubt. Jacob manipulates his family and deceives his father. Joseph's brothers commit a betrayal that seems impossible to repair. The book does not hide weakness. It puts it in full view and then asks what can still become possible afterward.

Yet the story does not end with these failures.

Instead, Genesis repeatedly shows transformation. Jacob becomes Israel after wrestling through his struggle and confronting his past. Joseph chooses forgiveness when he has the power to seek revenge. Families fractured by conflict find moments of reconciliation. The future is not easy, but it is not permanently locked by past failure.

Failure does not have to define the future. Change remains possible.

For readers navigating their own mistakes or broken circumstances, this theme is not sentimental. It is tactical. Genesis doesn't pretend the damage isn't real. It simply insists the damage is not always final. Redemption can begin even after the betrayal. Even after the loss. Even after the years you can't get back.

Redemption begins when individuals choose humility, forgiveness, and trust. It begins when people stop denying the wound and start telling the truth about it. It begins when responsibility replaces blame and when grace is treated as strength, not weakness.

Genesis closes with the descendants of Abraham preserved in Egypt during a time of famine. The covenant promise remains active even though its full realization still lies ahead. The story continues, and so does the possibility of restoration.

That may be the clearest reason Genesis still matters for modern life. It tells the truth about human failure without surrendering to despair. It names what breaks people and then shows that God still works with the broken.

The story continues. And so does the possibility of restoration.

Chapter 8

Modern Reflection

You intended to harm me, but God intended it for good to
accomplish what is now being done, the saving of many lives.
—Genesis 50:20

The stories of Genesis may be ancient, but the questions they raise
are surprisingly modern. Every generation wrestles with the same
underlying tensions: identity and ambition, loyalty and betrayal,
power and responsibility. Technology changes, cultures evolve,
and societies grow more complex, yet the fundamental struggles
of human life remain remarkably consistent.

Genesis captures these tensions through the lives of ordinary
people placed in extraordinary circumstances. Its characters
navigate family conflict, moral decisions, personal ambition, and
uncertain futures. Their stories unfold in deserts and ancient cities,
yet the emotional terrain they travel is familiar to readers today.

The world surrounding modern readers looks very different
from the world of Genesis. Communication moves instantly.
Global events unfold in real time. Entire identities can be built
and evaluated through digital platforms within moments.
Decisions are often made quickly, and the consequences can
spread far beyond what earlier generations could have imagined.

But time doesn't retire the human heart.

Beneath those differences lies something surprisingly familiar.
The deeper struggles described in Genesis have not disappeared.
Human beings still wrestle with questions about identity, power,
trust, ambition, family conflict, and the consequences of personal
decisions. The cultural setting may be ancient, but the emotional
and moral dynamics remain recognizable. The same patterns

continue to appear, even when the settings have changed beyond recognition.

When viewed through this lens, Genesis begins to feel less like distant history and more like a reflection of the world we already know. The stories describe people navigating the same tensions that individuals and communities face today. They reveal patterns of behavior that appear repeatedly across generations, which is why Genesis keeps finding people even when people aren't looking for it.

Ambition. Fear. Hope. Failure. Forgiveness.

These themes connect the ancient narrative to modern experience in powerful ways. They remind readers that while cultures evolve, human beings continue to ask the same deep questions: Who am I? What makes a life meaningful? How should power be used? What do I do with regret? Can broken things be restored?

Genesis does not answer those questions with abstract theory. It answers them through stories, and that is part of why the book remains so compelling. Stories bypass defenses. They don't just tell you what to think. They show you what happens. They let you watch a life unfold under pressure, then ask you what you would do if you were standing in that same moment.

Stories make the lesson personal. The tension becomes harder to dismiss.

The Search for Identity

Modern society places enormous pressure on individuals to define themselves through success, productivity, or recognition. From an early age, people are encouraged to pursue achievement and to measure their progress against the accomplishments of others. Educational success, professional advancement, financial stability, and public recognition often become the benchmarks by which individuals evaluate their worth.

Careers become central to identity.

In many environments, you're not asked who you are. You're asked what you do. And if you don't have an answer that sounds impressive, you feel it. That pressure doesn't stop at work. It bleeds into family expectations, social circles, and even church communities. People start tying value to their output, their income, their influence, their visible strength.

Social media and digital communication amplify these pressures by constantly displaying the achievements of others. Comparison becomes not only possible but constant. People are rarely allowed to simply live their lives. They are invited, and sometimes pressured, to perform them. You can be quietly faithful, quietly consistent, quietly loving—and still feel "behind" because your life doesn't look loud enough online.

When success arrives, identity may feel secure. When circumstances change, that sense of identity can unravel quickly. Careers shift. Opportunities disappear. Recognition fades. Roles that once felt permanent can dissolve faster than expected. A person who has built worth entirely on visible accomplishment may suddenly feel as though nothing stable remains.

When identity is built entirely upon achievement, it becomes unstable.

Genesis offers a different starting point. Before humanity accomplishes anything, the text describes human beings as created in the image of God. Identity appears before performance. Value exists before achievement. Creation comes first. That order matters because it means worth is not something you earn. It is something you receive.

This perspective challenges many assumptions present in modern culture. It suggests that worth cannot be measured solely by productivity, usefulness, or public success. Instead, identity rests on a deeper foundation that exists before accomplishment and remains intact even when achievements change. It also exposes the weakness of a life built only on applause.

That idea carries practical implications for everyday life. Individuals who understand their worth as grounded in creation rather than achievement often approach success differently. Victory becomes something to steward rather than something that defines personal value. Failure becomes a moment of learning rather than a collapse of identity. Success may still matter, but it is no longer ultimate. It becomes part of life, not the source of life.

The foundation remains stable. Achievement may change. Worth does not.

This perspective also changes how people see others. When identity is grounded in inherent dignity rather than visible accomplishment, people can no longer be reduced to output, status, or usefulness. Genesis insists that every human being carries weight and meaning before anyone else approves of them. It forces a different ethic: you don't treat people according to their résumé; you treat them according to their value.

Leadership and Character

Genesis also provides insight into the development of leadership. In many modern contexts, leadership is associated with visibility and authority. Titles, promotions, and positions of influence often become the primary markers of leadership. Those who hold power are assumed to be leaders, while those without formal authority may be overlooked.

Genesis presents a different pattern.

Joseph's story illustrates this clearly. Early in life, Joseph experiences circumstances that appear to move him far away from leadership. Betrayed by his brothers, he is sold into slavery and taken to Egypt. Later, he is falsely accused and imprisoned. From the outside, Joseph's life appears to be defined by injustice, obscurity, and misfortune.

Years pass in obscurity.

But those years are doing something. Joseph's character is being formed under pressure, where the mask comes off. Joseph develops discipline, wisdom, and integrity while serving in environments where recognition is minimal and circumstances are difficult. He learns how to act responsibly before he is given large-scale responsibility. He learns how to keep his footing when the ground keeps shifting.

He learns patience in rooms where nobody claps.

He learns restraint when power is taken away.

He learns consistency when circumstances are inconsistent.

These qualities eventually prepare him for leadership. When Joseph rises to authority in Egypt, he is not simply given power. He has been shaped by experience. His years of hardship have developed the resilience, patience, and foresight necessary to guide a nation through famine. The preparation came first. Authority came later.

This pattern appears frequently in modern leadership journeys. Many of the individuals who demonstrate the greatest integrity and resilience have passed through seasons of difficulty before assuming positions of influence. Hardship strips away illusion. It exposes motives. It reveals whether a person wants influence for service or for self-protection. It answers the quiet question: what kind of person are you when you have no leverage?

Adversity often reveals character. It also refines it.

Genesis suggests that leadership is not defined solely by authority but by the ability to act wisely and responsibly when opportunities arise. Titles may grant influence, but they do not create depth. Real leadership is often formed in private long before it is seen in public.

Power reveals character. Character determines how power is used.

That insight matters in homes, workplaces, churches, businesses, and public life. People may be promoted for competence, charisma, or force of will, but only character allows power to be used without corruption. Genesis reminds readers that leadership without formation is dangerous, and that quiet years are not wasted years when they are shaping the inner life.

Family Conflict

Few areas of modern life produce more emotional complexity than family relationships. Families carry expectations, loyalties, traditions, and shared histories that shape how individuals relate to one another. When trust is strong, families can become powerful sources of support and stability. When conflict develops, however, those same relationships can become sources of deep tension.

Misunderstandings formed early in life sometimes echo for decades.

Genesis portrays family conflict with striking honesty. The book does not attempt to present families as ideal environments where harmony always prevails. Instead, it acknowledges the tensions that often arise when human weakness enters relationships.

Cain and Abel demonstrate how jealousy can escalate into violence. Jacob and Esau reveal the damage that favoritism and deception can cause within a household. Joseph and his brothers illustrate how resentment can grow when perceived injustice remains unresolved. These stories feel familiar because similar dynamics still appear in modern families.

Competition between siblings. Struggles for parental approval. Long-standing grievances that shape future relationships.

Genesis does not romanticize these struggles. But it also does not present them as permanent. Reconciliation remains possible.

When Joseph finally confronts his brothers years after their betrayal, he possesses the power to punish them. Instead, he chooses forgiveness. His decision does not erase the past, but it opens the door to restoration. The family begins to heal, not because the wrong was insignificant, but because revenge is not allowed to become the future.

Modern families face similar crossroads. Bitterness can remain indefinitely, or individuals can choose a different direction. That choice does not make pain disappear, and it does not always restore a relationship to its former shape. But it can interrupt a cycle that would otherwise continue unchecked.

Forgiveness requires courage. It also requires humility.

Genesis reminds readers that healing often begins when someone chooses reconciliation over revenge, honesty over avoidance, and responsibility over self-protection. Family systems often remain stuck because everyone wants change without confession. Genesis offers a more honest path: name what happened, own what's yours, release what you don't control, and refuse to let the wound dictate the future.

Pride and Ambition

The story of Babel introduces another recurring human pattern: the desire to build identity through power and recognition. The builders of the tower attempt to construct a structure that reaches toward heaven. Their goal is not simply architectural achievement. They seek to establish a name for themselves and prevent their community from scattering across the earth.

They want security. They want influence. They want recognition.

The tower becomes a symbol of human ambition directed toward self-exaltation. Modern culture often reflects similar impulses. Organizations compete for influence and expansion. Individuals pursue recognition through achievement, wealth, status, and visibility. Entire societies sometimes measure success primarily through growth, control, and public reach.

Ambition itself is not condemned in Genesis. What the story warns against is ambition detached from humility.

Ambition can be productive when it is connected to purpose, service, and stewardship. But when success becomes the primary measure of worth, individuals and institutions may pursue achievement without considering its deeper consequences. They may begin to treat people as tools, compromise integrity for momentum, and call it "necessary." They may believe that scale equals truth, and that visibility equals righteousness.

History repeatedly confirms this pattern. Empires rise and fall. Institutions expand and decline. Personal accomplishments that once seemed permanent eventually fade. Babel is not only about ancient architecture. It is about the repeated human temptation to believe that scale, visibility, and control can secure identity.

Genesis reminds readers that ambition without humility often leads to collapse.

Purpose outweighs prestige.

This matters for careers, ministries, companies, and personal goals. People do not only need to ask, "Can I build this?" They must also ask, "Why am I building it?" Genesis suggests that the answer to that second question often determines whether what is built will endure or unravel.

Decisions and Consequences

One of the most consistent lessons throughout Genesis is the reality that decisions shape long-term outcomes. Life is rarely defined by a single dramatic moment. Instead, the direction of a life often emerges from the accumulation of small choices made over time.

Small choices accumulate.

Cain chooses anger rather than reconciliation. Jacob chooses deception rather than honesty. Joseph chooses integrity even when doing so brings personal cost. Each decision influences future events. Some choices produce immediate consequences.

Others shape circumstances in subtle ways that only become visible years later.

Relationships, careers, and communities often reflect the results of decisions made long before the outcomes become apparent.

Modern life presents similar moments. A conversation handled poorly can damage a relationship for years. A moment of integrity can build trust that lasts a lifetime. A small compromise may create consequences far beyond the original situation. A habit tolerated in private may eventually determine what happens in public.

Genesis encourages readers to recognize the weight carried by everyday decisions. Many people imagine lives are altered mainly through dramatic turning points, but Genesis pays close attention to quieter moments: the moment a boundary is crossed, the moment resentment is entertained, the moment fear becomes deception, the moment mercy is chosen instead of revenge.

The direction of a life is rarely determined by a single event. It is shaped by patterns.

This insight is both sobering and hopeful. It is sobering because small compromises matter. But it is hopeful because small acts of wisdom matter too. Faithfulness is rarely glamorous in Genesis. It is often expressed through ordinary choices made consistently over time, even when no one notices.

Hope in Broken Circumstances

Perhaps the most encouraging reflection offered by Genesis is the idea that broken situations can still lead to unexpected outcomes. Joseph's life illustrates this reality vividly. Betrayal leads to slavery. Slavery leads to imprisonment. Each stage of his life appears to move further away from the dreams he once shared with his family.

From the outside, the story looks like a collapse.

Yet those same events eventually place him in a position where he can preserve life during a devastating famine. The narrative does not suggest that suffering is desirable. It does not romanticize betrayal or injustice. But it does suggest that suffering does not always determine the final outcome.

That distinction matters.

Many modern readers encounter seasons that feel uncertain or discouraging. Careers change unexpectedly. Relationships fracture. Plans collapse. Health falters. Loss arrives without warning. These moments can create the sense that the future has been permanently altered.

Genesis offers a different perspective.

Difficult circumstances do not necessarily define the final chapter of a story.

Transformation remains possible, even in the middle of hardship and even when the path forward is unclear. Joseph cannot see what his suffering will one day mean while he is in the pit or the prison. The meaning becomes visible only later. That does not remove the pain, but it does change the final interpretation.

The possibility of restoration remains open.

This is one of Genesis's deepest gifts to modern readers. It refuses denial and refuses despair. It tells the truth about suffering while insisting that suffering does not hold ultimate authority over the outcome. Hope in Genesis is not naïve optimism. It is the disciplined conviction that broken circumstances do not always get the final word.

And that conviction still speaks with force today.

Chapter 9

Reflection Questions

Then the Lord said to Cain, "Where is your brother Abel?"
"I don't know," he replied. "Am I my brother's keeper?"
—Genesis 4:9

Genesis invites readers not only to understand the story but also to examine their own lives in light of its themes. The narratives contained in the book describe individuals who faced choices, struggles, and uncertainties that continue to appear in every generation. The details of daily life may differ from one era to another, but the deeper human questions remain remarkably consistent.

The circumstances may differ.

The underlying questions remain the same.

Throughout Genesis, people wrestle with identity, responsibility, ambition, trust, and reconciliation. Their experiences reveal patterns that still shape human life today. Reflecting on these patterns allows readers to move beyond simply observing the story and begin considering how its lessons apply to their own decisions, relationships, fears, and hopes.

The following questions are not meant to produce quick answers. They are meant to encourage thoughtful reflection. Some of the most important insights in life arrive slowly. They emerge not from rushing toward resolution, but from sitting honestly with what is true.

Reflection takes patience.

It also takes courage.

Genesis does not ask readers merely to admire or analyze its characters from a safe distance. It asks them to recognize themselves in the story. It invites them to consider where they are standing in relation to the same tensions that shaped Adam and Eve, Cain and Abel, Abraham, Jacob, and Joseph. The goal is not guilt for its own sake. The goal is clarity.

And clarity often begins with the right questions.

Identity and Purpose

Where do you currently draw your sense of identity—from achievements, relationships, status, or something deeper?

Genesis begins with the declaration that humanity is created in the image of God. This idea places identity at the very foundation of human existence. Before Adam and Eve accomplish anything, before they cultivate the garden, establish families, or influence the future, their value is already established.

They are created with purpose.

Modern culture often approaches identity differently. Many people measure their worth through accomplishments, recognition, or social visibility. Careers, educational achievements, financial success, physical appearance, and public reputation frequently become the benchmarks through which individuals evaluate themselves.

Success can create a strong sense of identity.

Failure can threaten it.

This creates a fragile way of living. When worth depends entirely on performance, a person is only as secure as the latest outcome. Achievements can disappear. Circumstances can change. Recognition fades. What once felt permanent can vanish quickly.

A deeper foundation is necessary.

Genesis challenges the modern habit of building identity on external results by suggesting that identity must begin before achievement. If human worth depends entirely on performance, then identity will always remain unstable. But if worth begins in creation, then success and failure can be interpreted differently.

Success becomes something to steward.

Failure becomes something to learn from.

Identity remains intact.

Reflecting on this question invites readers to consider what currently carries the most weight in their self-understanding. Do they feel valuable only when they are productive? Do they feel secure only when others approve of them? Are they living as though accomplishment must constantly justify their existence?

Genesis offers a steadier answer. Human worth is not an accident, and it is not something earned after the fact. It is present from the beginning. The challenge for modern readers is not merely to agree with that idea intellectually, but to actually live from it.

That may require honest reevaluation.

It may require letting go of false measures.

It may require learning to see yourself with more humility and more dignity at the same time.

Decisions and Consequences

What recent decision in your life may shape your future more than you realize?

Genesis repeatedly demonstrates how small decisions can influence the direction of entire lives. Many of the most significant turning points in the narrative emerge from moments that appear ordinary at first glance. A conversation, an act of deception, a surrender to anger, a choice to trust, a refusal to wait—these moments accumulate.

Cain's anger begins as an emotional response but ultimately leads to violence. Jacob's deception secures an immediate advantage but creates years of separation and conflict. Joseph's decision to maintain integrity in difficult circumstances eventually positions him to lead during a time of crisis.

The stories illustrate a consistent pattern.

Choices accumulate.

A single decision rarely determines the entire course of a life. Instead, patterns of behavior develop over time. Small actions form habits, and habits gradually shape character. Character then influences the way future decisions are made.

Modern life often moves quickly, making it easy to treat decisions as temporary or isolated. But Genesis slows the reader down. It shows how a moment that feels small can become the beginning of something far larger. A conversation handled poorly may damage a relationship for years. A moment of dishonesty may create instability that spreads into multiple areas of life. A quiet act of integrity may build trust that opens opportunities much later.

Consequences are often delayed.

That is part of what makes them easy to underestimate.

Reflecting on recent decisions can help readers recognize the direction in which their lives are moving. What habits are being reinforced? What patterns are being built? Where is compromise beginning to feel normal? Where is courage beginning to grow?

The path forward is often determined by the habits people cultivate today.

This question is especially important because people often imagine that the future will be shaped by dramatic moments alone. Genesis suggests otherwise. More often, the future is shaped by repeated choices made in ordinary circumstances. The issue is not only what decision was made, but what kind of person that decision is helping someone become.

That makes reflection practical, not abstract.

It helps identify the direction beneath the behavior.

Conflict and Reconciliation

Are there relationships in your life where forgiveness or humility could open the door to healing?

Family conflict appears repeatedly throughout Genesis. Rivalry between siblings, favoritism among parents, and unresolved resentment create tension that influences entire generations. The book is uncommonly honest about how easily relationships can fracture, especially when pride and insecurity are left unaddressed.

Cain and Abel represent the tragic consequences of jealousy. Jacob and Esau demonstrate how deception can fracture a family for years. Joseph and his brothers reveal how resentment can grow when perceived injustice remains unresolved.

Yet Genesis also includes moments of reconciliation.

Jacob eventually returns to face the brother he wronged. Joseph chooses forgiveness rather than revenge when his brothers come seeking food during the famine. These moments do not erase the past, but they create a new future. They show that while injury may be real, it does not have to have the final word.

Reconciliation requires courage.

It often begins when one person is willing to approach a difficult relationship with humility rather than defensiveness. That does not mean pretending nothing happened. It does not require minimizing harm. It means becoming willing to step out of the cycle of retaliation, silence, or self-protection and move toward truth.

Forgiveness does not always restore every relationship to its previous form. Some wounds require time, distance, boundaries, or wisdom in order to heal. Genesis does not portray reconciliation as easy or simplistic. But it does suggest that healing becomes possible when people stop allowing old injuries to dictate every future interaction.

Reflecting on this question invites readers to consider whether unresolved conflict is shaping their lives in ways they may not fully recognize. Is bitterness quietly hardening into identity? Is pride keeping a conversation from happening? Is fear making honesty feel too risky?

Healing sometimes begins with a single step.

Sometimes that step is confession.

Sometimes it is listening.

Sometimes it is choosing not to keep rehearsing the same grievance.

Genesis reminds readers that reconciliation is rarely automatic. It is chosen. And while not every relationship can be fully restored, many remain broken simply because neither side is willing to move first.

Reflection helps reveal whether that may be true in your own life.

Ambition and Humility

How do you balance ambition with the humility necessary to remain grounded?

Ambition appears frequently in Genesis. Individuals seek influence, recognition, security, and significance in ways that sometimes lead to conflict or unintended consequences. The book does not ignore human aspiration. It recognizes that people want their lives to matter and that they often seek to build something lasting.

The builders of Babel pursue a project designed to elevate their reputation and consolidate power. Their ambition reflects a desire to control their destiny without relying on God. The tower becomes a symbol of pride, not because building is wrong, but because self-exaltation has become the true motive beneath the work.

Genesis does not condemn ambition entirely. The desire to build, create, lead, and improve the world can produce remarkable achievements. Innovation, exploration, and leadership often arise from individuals who are motivated to accomplish something meaningful.

Ambition becomes problematic when it disconnects from humility.

When success becomes the primary measure of worth, individuals may begin making decisions that prioritize recognition over responsibility. Power can become an end in itself rather than a means of serving others. A person may still use good language about impact or purpose while being driven mainly by the need to be seen, validated, or remembered.

Humility acts as a stabilizing force.

It reminds individuals that success is rarely the result of personal effort alone. Opportunities, relationships, timing, and grace all play roles in shaping outcomes. Humility does not destroy ambition. It purifies it. It keeps the desire to accomplish from turning into the need to dominate.

Reflecting on this question encourages readers to examine their motivations. Why are you pursuing what you are pursuing? What kind of recognition are you hoping to receive? What would happen to your sense of worth if the work mattered but no one praised you for it?

Purpose provides direction.

Humility provides balance.

Without humility, ambition often hardens into pride. Without purpose, ambition becomes scattered and restless. Genesis encourages readers to pursue meaningful work while remaining aware that the self can quietly become the center of that work if humility is absent.

This question is not only for public leaders. It applies to anyone building something—career, ministry, family, reputation, business, platform, or legacy. The issue is not whether you are building, but what is governing the heart while you build.

Trust and Uncertainty

In what areas of your life are you being asked to move forward without having all the answers?

Uncertainty appears throughout the narrative of Genesis. Abraham's journey illustrates this reality most clearly. When God calls him to leave his homeland, the destination is not immediately revealed. Abraham is asked to begin traveling before he fully understands where the journey will lead.

Faith begins with movement.

Abraham steps forward despite uncertainty.

Many people encounter similar experiences during different stages of life. Career changes, personal transitions, unexpected challenges, and closed doors often create moments when the future appears unclear. Plans shift. Certainty disappears. The path that once seemed obvious becomes difficult to read.

In these moments, individuals may feel pressure to delay action until every detail becomes visible. But Genesis suggests that meaningful journeys often require movement before complete clarity emerges. Abraham's story unfolds gradually. The promise develops over years and even generations. Much of what is promised is not immediately seen.

Trust, in this context, does not mean ignoring uncertainty. It means recognizing that progress sometimes requires stepping forward even when the entire path cannot yet be seen. It means refusing to confuse uncertainty with abandonment. It means choosing obedience without demanding total control.

This question encourages readers to examine whether uncertainty is preventing them from moving toward meaningful opportunities or responsibilities. Are you waiting for guarantees that life rarely provides? Are you resisting a necessary step because the full outcome remains hidden? Are you treating trust as something you will practice later, once risk has been removed?

Clarity often grows with movement.

The next step sometimes becomes visible only after the previous step has been taken.

Genesis presents trust not as passivity, but as willing movement under incomplete understanding. That makes this question especially relevant in a world where people often want certainty before commitment, comfort before obedience, and proof before surrender.

Sometimes, the most honest answer is that you do not know where the path leads.

But you may still know the next step.

Reflection Is a Form of Honesty

Reflection is not merely an intellectual exercise. It is a process of examining how the patterns revealed in Genesis intersect with the realities of everyday life. The stories recorded in the book do more than describe ancient events. They illuminate decisions, relationships, motivations, and hopes that continue to shape human experience.

The same questions still matter.

The answers continue to unfold.

Taking time to reflect means refusing to stay on the surface. It means allowing the text to move from observation into examination. It means letting Genesis ask something of the reader rather than remaining a story about other people in another time.

That takes honesty.

It also takes patience, because some of the clearest answers do not come immediately. They emerge over time as readers begin to see where the story of Genesis overlaps with the story they are currently living.

And that is where reflection becomes transformation.

Chapter 10

Five Lessons from Genesis for Modern Life

Abram believed the Lord, and he credited it to him as
righteousness.
—Genesis 15:6

Genesis covers centuries of human history and introduces many individuals whose lives unfold across complex circumstances. The narrative moves from creation to corruption, from covenant to conflict, from betrayal to forgiveness, and from famine to preservation. It is a book of beginnings, but it is also a book of patterns—patterns that repeat because the human heart has not changed as quickly as human technology.

That matters because the temptation is to assume we've evolved past the old problems. We have better tools. Better systems. Better medicine. Faster communication. More comfort. But Genesis keeps pulling the mask off and showing what still drives us underneath the surface: pride, fear, hunger for significance, the impulse to control, and the tendency to break trust and then act surprised when trust is hard to rebuild.

The characters in Genesis are not presented as flawless heroes. They are people navigating uncertainty, ambition, fear, loyalty, loss, and hope. They make courageous choices at times. They also make destructive ones. Genesis does not sanitize that reality. It puts the human condition on the page and lets the reader feel the weight of it.

Their experiences reveal patterns that continue to shape human life today.

Although the world has changed dramatically since the time these stories were first told, the underlying lessons remain remarkably relevant. Modern life has more speed, more convenience, and more noise. It also has the same insecurity, the same rivalry, the same craving for approval, and the same tendency to confuse achievement with identity. People still chase blessings without surrender, outcomes without obedience, influence without formation.

Genesis explains why that happens. It also shows what can happen next.

Several insights stand out repeatedly. These are not quick slogans. They are lessons forged through choices and consequences, through relationships that fracture, and through moments where grace interrupts what should have been the end of the story. Genesis teaches with blood, not theory. It teaches through fathers and sons, brothers and betrayal, deserts and delays. And the lessons land because they are still our lessons.

1. Identity Comes Before Achievement

Genesis begins with a declaration that establishes the foundation for human identity: human beings are created in the image of God. This statement appears before any accomplishment occurs. Before humanity builds cities, develops culture, achieves progress, or proves anything, identity is already defined.

Creation comes first. Achievement comes later.

That order carries significant meaning. It suggests that human worth does not originate from productivity, intelligence, social status, physical strength, beauty, or public approval. Dignity exists because human life itself is intentional. You do not earn your right to matter. You have it from the beginning.

Value precedes accomplishment.

In many modern societies, identity is often constructed in the opposite direction. People define themselves through careers, achievements, financial success, appearance, influence, personal brand, or recognition. The question becomes, "What have you done?" and then, "What does that say about you?" When that framework runs the show, self-worth rises and falls with outcomes. It becomes performance-based living with spiritual consequences.

Success strengthens identity. Failure threatens it.

That is a volatile way to live. A promotion can feel like proof of worth. A setback can feel like personal collapse. A season of momentum can create confidence that is actually dependence. People begin to chase validation instead of purpose. They become driven by fear of losing status rather than by a steady understanding of who they are. They stop stewarding success and start being owned by it.

Genesis proposes a different perspective. If identity rests solely on accomplishment, identity becomes fragile. Circumstances change. Careers evolve. Recognition fades. Bodies age. Markets shift. Organizations restructure. Friends move. Platforms disappear. People forget. And what happens to you if your identity was stored in what people remember?

Achievements may shift over time. Human dignity does not.

Understanding this principle reshapes how individuals approach both success and failure. Success becomes an opportunity to steward influence responsibly rather than a source of personal validation. Failure becomes a moment of growth, correction, and learning rather than a collapse of identity. That does not mean failure is painless. It means failure is not final in terms of worth.

Identity grounded in creation remains stable, even when circumstances change.

Modern life desperately needs this. People are burning out not only from work but from the belief that they must constantly prove their value. Many aren't tired because the load is heavy; they're tired because their soul believes the load is the receipt that justifies their existence. Genesis offers relief without lowering the standard of responsibility. It anchors worth deep enough that a storm cannot easily uproot it.

And that changes everything: how you lead, how you parent, how you compete, how you lose, how you recover, how you treat other people. If identity is received, not earned, then you can finally stop performing for oxygen.

2. Freedom Carries Responsibility

Another lesson that appears repeatedly in Genesis involves the relationship between freedom and responsibility. From the beginning, humanity is given freedom. Adam and Eve are placed in the garden with the ability to explore, cultivate, and enjoy the environment around them. Only one boundary exists, represented by the command concerning the tree in the center of the garden.

The command introduces a fundamental reality: freedom requires trust.

Freedom is not the absence of limits. It is the ability to live meaningfully within the right limits. In Genesis, the boundary is not presented as cruelty. It is presented as a moral line that preserves relationship and order. Crossing that line is more than breaking a rule. It is choosing independence over trust, self-definition over guidance, appetite over obedience.

When Adam and Eve cross that boundary, the consequences extend far beyond the immediate moment. Their decision fractures relationship with God, disrupts harmony between the man and the woman, alters their relationship with the natural world, and introduces fear, shame, blame, and separation. Work becomes difficult. Trust becomes fragile. Mortality becomes inevitable. The human heart becomes divided—wanting what is good, yet turning toward what destroys.

The narrative illustrates how a single decision can influence the future.

This pattern continues throughout the rest of Genesis. Cain chooses anger rather than reconciliation, and the result is violence and exile. Jacob chooses deception rather than honesty, and the result is years of conflict, fear, and relational damage. Joseph's brothers choose betrayal rather than loyalty, and the consequences echo through the entire family. Joseph chooses integrity even when it brings hardship, and that choice shapes his future influence. Freedom is real, but it is never weightless.

Each decision shapes the course of events that follow.

Modern life presents similar moments. Individuals encounter situations where choices appear small or temporary. A compromise feels minor. A lie feels like a shortcut. Avoiding a hard conversation feels easier than confronting it. A boundary crossed "just once" becomes a pattern. In the moment, the decision seems contained. Over time, the consequences spread.

A single conversation may strengthen or damage a relationship.

A moment of integrity may build trust that lasts for years.

A repeated compromise may form a habit that reshapes character.

Freedom always includes responsibility.

Genesis also shows that people are rarely destroyed by one catastrophic decision alone. More often, they drift because of repeated small decisions. Choices form habits. Habits shape character. Character influences destiny. That is not fatalism; it is moral reality. Genesis teaches that life has weight, and that freedom is never neutral.

Freedom can build a life. Freedom can break a life. The difference is whether responsibility is embraced or avoided.

And if you want to see this in real time, you don't have to look far. Watch what happens in a marriage when small honesty disappears. Watch what happens in a business when small compromises become culture. Watch what happens in a leader when private shortcuts become public scandal. Genesis is ancient, but it reads like today because it is describing the same mechanics of the heart.

3. Pride Eventually Collapses

Genesis reveals the dangers of pride when ambition becomes disconnected from humility. The story of Babel illustrates this lesson vividly. The builders of the tower seek to construct a structure that will secure their reputation and prevent their communities from dispersing across the earth. Their project reflects a desire for recognition and control.

They want to build something that will define their identity.

The tower becomes a monument to human ambition and self-exaltation. The deeper problem is not building; it is building for the wrong reason. They are not pursuing purpose. They are pursuing self-importance and security through control. Their identity is being anchored in what they can construct rather than in what they are called to steward. Their unity is not rooted in humility or shared obedience. It is rooted in shared pride.

The project collapses when communication breaks down, and the people scatter. The effort to establish lasting significance through pride ultimately undermines itself. Genesis portrays this not as random sabotage but as a reality check: pride cannot hold a society together, because pride cannot hold a soul together.

The pattern repeats throughout history.

Empires rise. Empires fall. Institutions expand. Institutions decline. Achievements that once seemed permanent eventually fade. Individuals who build their identity on dominance or visibility eventually face the limits of time, resistance, and consequence. Pride always overpromises. It says, "This will make you secure." Then it leaves you exposed.

Genesis does not suggest that ambition itself is wrong. Human creativity, exploration, and innovation often arise from the desire to build something meaningful. Progress frequently depends on individuals willing to imagine new possibilities and pursue difficult goals. Genesis is not anti-building. It is anti-idolatry.

Ambition becomes dangerous when it loses connection with humility.

When success becomes the primary measure of identity, individuals and societies may pursue recognition at the expense of wisdom. Pride creates the illusion that control is permanent and that outcomes justify whatever methods were used to obtain them. That is how good intentions become corruption. That is how leaders start believing they're the exception to the rules they demand for everyone else.

Genesis reminds readers that humility provides stability. Pride isolates. Humility sustains.

Humility does not mean passivity. It means clarity. It means remembering you are not the center of the story. It means understanding that power is given for stewardship, not self-worship. It means recognizing that success can be a test as much as failure is.

Pride builds fast. Humility builds deep. Genesis warns that what is built fast, high, and loud often collapses harder.

And the collapse isn't always external. Sometimes the collapse is internal: a leader loses his soul while keeping his title. A person gains the world and becomes someone they don't respect. Babel is not only about buildings. It's about the quiet corruption of the heart when identity gets tied to being impressive.

4. Integrity Shapes the Future

Another lesson woven throughout Genesis involves the long-term influence of integrity. Joseph's life illustrates this principle clearly. After being betrayed by his brothers and sold into slavery, Joseph faces circumstances that could easily lead to bitterness or moral compromise. He has every excuse to quit caring about truth and right living. He has been treated unjustly. He has been stripped of agency. He could argue that integrity is for people who have options.

Instead, he continues to act with honesty and diligence.

Even when doing so appears costly.

He works faithfully in a household where he has no power. He refuses to compromise even when it would have benefited him. He endures false accusation and imprisonment without abandoning integrity. The text does not portray him as emotionless or untouched by suffering. It portrays him as consistent in his character despite suffering. He does not let pain decide who he becomes.

Over time, that consistency becomes the foundation of his leadership.

When Joseph eventually rises to authority in Egypt, he is prepared to guide the nation through a devastating famine. His leadership preserves countless lives, including the family that once betrayed him. The integrity formed in adversity becomes influential later. His trustworthiness is not sudden. It has been tested. He becomes a man people can rely on when the stakes are high because he was faithful when the stakes seemed pointless.

Integrity formed during adversity becomes influential later.

Modern life presents similar opportunities. People face moments where ethical shortcuts appear tempting. Dishonesty may promise immediate advantage. Integrity may require patience, restraint, and the willingness to accept short-term loss for long-term stability. And often the cost of integrity is not dramatic; it's quiet. It's being overlooked. It's losing a deal. It's refusing the shortcut. It's doing the right thing with no applause.

Genesis suggests that long-term outcomes are often shaped by decisions made when no recognition is guaranteed. That is where integrity is forged—when doing the right thing costs something, and when nobody is watching. Integrity may appear costly in the moment. But it builds trust. Trust builds influence. Influence creates the possibility of meaningful leadership.

This applies far beyond leadership roles. It applies to friendships, marriage, parenting, business, ministry, and private life. Integrity is not only about avoiding scandal. It is about becoming the kind of person whose presence is safe, whose word carries weight, and whose decisions can be trusted under pressure. It is about being the same person in the dark as you are in the light.

Integrity does not make life easy. It makes life solid.

Genesis shows that solidity matters more than speed. In a culture addicted to momentum, integrity is the slow path that keeps you alive long enough to finish well.

5. Redemption Is Always Possible

Perhaps the most powerful lesson in Genesis is the recurring possibility of redemption. Nearly every major character in the book experiences failure. Abraham struggles with fear and doubt. Jacob manipulates his family through deception. Joseph's brothers commit an act of betrayal that seems impossible to repair.

The narrative does not excuse these failures. It names them.

Genesis is honest about sin. It is honest about damage. It is honest about consequences. It never asks the reader to call darkness light. But it also refuses to conclude that failure is the final chapter.

Yet Genesis does not end with those failures.

Instead, the story repeatedly moves toward restoration. Jacob returns home after years of separation and confronts his past. Joseph chooses forgiveness rather than revenge when his brothers stand before him in need. Families fractured by jealousy and deception gradually find moments of healing. People change. Not perfectly. Not instantly. But genuinely.

Redemption does not erase the past. But it changes the future.

Genesis suggests that failure does not have to define a life. Transformation remains possible even after serious mistakes, broken trust, and long seasons of loss. That does not mean consequences disappear. Genesis is honest about consequences. But it also shows that consequences do not eliminate the possibility of a new direction.

This message resonates in modern life because people carry regret. They carry shame. They carry the memory of what they said, what they did, what they failed to do, and what they lost. Many assume the future has been permanently limited by past decisions. Some even build an identity out of their worst moment, as if the wound is the only true thing about them.

Genesis offers a different perspective: change remains possible.

Restoration can begin even in situations that appear hopeless. Forgiveness can be chosen even when revenge feels justified. A person can become different—not by pretending the past never happened, but by facing it and stepping forward with humility. Redemption is not denial. Redemption is truth plus grace moving forward.

The past influences the present. But it does not have to determine the future.

That is not sentimental optimism. It is hard-earned hope. Genesis lays it down again and again: God's purposes are not fragile, and human failure is not the final word.

The Lessons Hold

Genesis closes with a family preserved during famine, living in Egypt, and carrying the promise that began with Abraham. The full outcome of that promise has not yet appeared, but the direction of the story is clear. Despite human failure, the narrative continues to move toward restoration.

That is why Genesis still speaks.

Identity begins with creation.

Freedom requires responsibility.

Pride eventually collapses.

Integrity shapes the future.

And redemption remains possible.

Those lessons are not trapped in ancient history. They are alive because we are still living in the same human story—still making choices, still dealing with consequences, still longing for meaning, and still needing grace strong enough to carry what we cannot fix on our own.

Closing Reflection

Then Joseph said to his brothers, "I am about to die. But God will surely come to your aid and take you up out of this land to the land he promised on oath to Abraham, Isaac, and Jacob."
—Genesis 50:24

Genesis begins with creation and ends with a family preserved during famine. Between those two moments lies a sweeping narrative that stretches across generations and landscapes. The story moves from the formation of the universe to the struggles of individual families navigating fear, ambition, betrayal, reconciliation, and hope. It starts with the language of light and oceans, then gradually turns toward the language of hearts and homes.

What begins with cosmic scale slowly narrows to human scale.

Stars and oceans give way to conversations around tents, strained family relationships, difficult decisions, and moments where ordinary people must choose whether to trust, resist, forgive, or take control. The narrative moves from the vastness of creation to the intimacy of human experience, showing how the story of the world eventually becomes the story of a family. That shift is intentional. Genesis not only explains what happened long ago. It's showing where the fracture lives now: inside human beings, inside relationships, inside communities.

Along the way, Genesis confronts the reality of human weakness while also revealing the persistence of hope. It does not flatter the reader. It does not pretend that the human problem is minor, temporary, or easily fixed by education, structure, or time. It names what is broken and shows how quickly it spreads.

The book does not present an idealized version of humanity. Its characters are not flawless heroes who always act with wisdom and courage. Instead, they are deeply recognizable individuals wrestling with the same tensions that appear in every generation—tensions you can still see in your own home, your own decisions, and your own internal battles.

Fear influences decisions.

Jealousy disrupts relationships.

Ambition creates conflict.

Trust is broken.

And yet the narrative never abandons the possibility of restoration. That is the steady heartbeat beneath the mess. Genesis refuses to surrender to despair, even when the evidence would seem to justify it.

This honesty is one of the reasons Genesis continues to resonate across centuries. The book acknowledges that human life contains both dignity and brokenness. People are capable of creativity, loyalty, courage, and love. At the same time, they are capable of pride, deception, violence, and betrayal. Genesis does not pick one side of the human story. It holds both in the same frame.

Both realities appear side by side.

Genesis refuses to pretend that humanity is either purely noble or purely corrupt. Instead, it portrays human beings as complex creatures—capable of building and destroying, of loving and wounding, of seeking God while also resisting Him. It shows how someone can want a blessing and still refuse to surrender. It shows how people can know what is right and still reach for what is wrong.

That tension remains true today.

The Beginning of the Story

Genesis begins with a world created in order and harmony. Humanity is placed within that world with freedom and responsibility. The garden represents the possibility of life lived in trust and relationship with God. In that setting, work is meaningful, relationships are whole, and creation itself reflects stability and beauty. Nothing is scrambling for identity. Nothing is trying to prove itself. Everything belongs.

Everything begins as it should be.

But that harmony does not last. Genesis wastes no time showing how quickly trust can be replaced by suspicion, and how quickly innocence can be replaced by shame. The story turns on a decision that looks small on the surface but carries lethal weight underneath.

A single decision alters the course of the story. Adam and Eve chose independence over trust, believing they could define good and evil for themselves rather than receiving that definition from the Creator. The choice appears small in the moment—one boundary crossed, one desire justified, one act that seems manageable. But Genesis treats it as what it is: the beginning of a new orientation of the heart.

The garden is lost.

Relationships fracture. Work becomes difficult. Shame enters human experience. Fear replaces openness. Mortality becomes an unavoidable reality. The human impulse to hide begins, and with it comes the impulse to blame. Genesis shows that brokenness is not only about consequences outside us; it's about distortion inside us.

The narrative does not hide these consequences. Genesis refuses to soften the impact of that first decision. Instead, it traces how the effects spread through families, communities, and cultures. The fracture introduced in Eden does not remain isolated. It becomes the beginning of a pattern—one that repeats because the root problem repeats.

Brokenness multiplies.

The Spread of Brokenness

Violence emerges quickly in the story of Cain and Abel. What begins as jealousy grows into anger, and anger becomes the first murder recorded in the biblical narrative. The tragedy is not distant. It happens within the first family. Genesis shows that the first battlefield is not between nations. It is between brothers.

The damage deepens.

As generations pass, corruption expands until the world described in the days of Noah becomes defined by destructive behavior. Violence becomes normal. Trust erodes. Communities are shaped by selfishness and power rather than wisdom and restraint. The text describes moral collapse not as a rare event but as a cultural atmosphere—something in the air people breathe.

The flood represents both judgment and cleansing.

Yet even after the waters recede, the deeper problem remains unresolved. Humanity begins again, but the human heart has not fundamentally changed. New land does not create a new nature. A reset does not produce restoration by itself. Genesis refuses the fantasy that circumstances alone can fix what is wrong within us.

The story of Babel illustrates how quickly ambition returns. People attempt to secure their identity and power by building a tower that symbolizes control and reputation. Their goal is not just to create; it is to dominate. They want unity on their terms, significance on their terms, security on their terms.

Humanity once again seeks to define itself apart from God.

The brokenness becomes clear. Genesis does not pretend that progress alone will fix what is wrong. The book recognizes something deeper at work—a moral fracture that cannot be solved simply by building better cities, organizing stronger societies, or producing smarter systems.

Something within humanity needs restoration.

The Quiet Movement of Grace

Yet even within these moments of failure, the story continues moving forward. This is where Genesis becomes more than a diagnosis. It becomes direction. The damage is real, but the narrative does not stall. Judgment appears, yes—but mercy appears too. Consequences unfold, but the story does not end in collapse.

Noah survives the flood and becomes the beginning of a new generation. Abraham receives a promise that his family will become a blessing to the world. Jacob, despite his manipulation and deception, encounters a transformation during his struggle with God. Joseph, betrayed and enslaved, rises to leadership and ultimately saves the very family that once rejected him.

Grace appears repeatedly.

Sometimes quietly. Sometimes dramatically.

The persistence of this grace becomes one of the defining features of Genesis. Human failure never completely stops the movement of the story. Even when individuals make destructive choices, the possibility of restoration continues to appear. Genesis is clear: the story does not depend on human perfection. It depends on divine faithfulness.

The promise continues.

Genesis suggests that redemption does not advance because people suddenly become perfect. It advances because grace continues to meet people within their imperfections. Again and again, the narrative shows that God remains engaged with humanity even when humanity repeatedly moves in the wrong direction. The presence of God does not disappear when people fail. He confronts. He corrects. He guides. He continues.

The story keeps moving.

Ordinary People in an Extraordinary Story

Genesis also reveals how the larger story of humanity often unfolds through ordinary individuals rather than extraordinary heroes. The central figures in the narrative are not kings ruling vast empires or warriors conquering nations. They are not spiritual superheroes. They are families—messy, anxious, divided families trying to survive and trying to make sense of what God is doing.

They are families.

Abraham struggles with fear and uncertainty. Jacob deceives his own family and spends years dealing with the consequences of his actions. Joseph's brothers commit an act of betrayal that nearly destroys their household. These people are flawed. They are inconsistent. They are sometimes courageous and sometimes afraid. They are capable of faith in one moment and compromise in the next.

Yet these same people become participants in a larger narrative that extends far beyond their individual lives.

The book suggests that the unfolding story of redemption does not depend on human perfection. It depends on divine persistence. That is not a soft truth. It is a strong one. It means God's purposes are not fragile. It means failure is not final. It means broken people can still be used without pretending they were never broken.

This insight is deeply encouraging for modern readers. Many people assume that meaningful lives require flawless decisions or uninterrupted success. Failure, regret, and broken relationships can create the sense that the future has been permanently altered.

Genesis challenges that assumption.

The characters who shape the story are often the same individuals who make serious mistakes along the way. Failure does not remove them from the narrative. Instead, it becomes part of the process through which transformation occurs. Consequences remain, but so does calling. The wound becomes a place where humility can finally grow.

The Possibility of Redemption

One of the most powerful messages in Genesis is the repeated possibility of redemption. Even in moments that appear final, the story continues to move toward restoration. Genesis does not promise pain-free outcomes. It does not claim that betrayal doesn't matter. It doesn't minimize grief. It simply refuses to let the worst moment be the last word.

Jacob returns home after years of separation and confronts the brother he once deceived. Joseph chooses forgiveness rather than revenge when his brothers stand before him in need. Families fractured by jealousy and betrayal gradually find moments of healing. These are not sentimental endings. They are costly choices—choices that require humility, restraint, and courage.

Redemption does not erase the past.

But it changes the future.

Genesis suggests that failure does not have to define a life. Transformation remains possible even after serious mistakes or painful consequences. The past influences the present, but it does not necessarily determine the future. Redemption remains possible—not because people can time-travel and undo what they did, but because God can build a different future out of damaged ground.

Redemption remains possible.

Even after betrayal.

Even after loss.

Even after years of wandering.

This message speaks directly to modern readers who carry regret or disappointment. Many people believe that the story of their lives has already been limited by previous decisions or broken circumstances. They assume their best chapter is behind them. Genesis does not agree.

Genesis offers a different perspective.

The story is not finished.

A Story That Continues

The final chapters of Genesis bring the narrative to a quiet but significant moment. Joseph's family settles in Egypt after surviving a devastating famine. The immediate crisis has passed. The family has been preserved. Yet the larger promise given to Abraham has not yet been fully realized.

The story pauses.

But it does not end.

The descendants of this family will eventually grow into a nation, and their journey will continue through the events described in the rest of the biblical narrative. Genesis, therefore, functions as both a beginning and an invitation. It introduces the questions that the rest of Scripture will continue to explore.

Why is the world broken?

Can humanity be restored?

How does redemption unfold within the complexity of human history?

Genesis does not answer every question completely. Instead, it establishes the direction of the story. Creation began with purpose. Humanity introduced brokenness. Yet hope continues to move forward. That movement becomes the thread that ties the entire biblical narrative together. The promise does not disappear. It continues through generations.

The promise persists even when people don't.

The Story Is Still Unfolding

The narrative closes with a quiet reminder that the future remains open. The world is still marked by both beauty and brokenness. Human beings still carry dignity alongside weakness. Families still struggle with conflict and reconciliation. Ambition still wrestles with humility. Faith still competes with fear. Control still tempts the heart.

But hope remains present.

Genesis invites readers not only to observe the story but also to recognize themselves within it. The same tensions, decisions, and questions continue to shape human lives today. The story that began in creation and continued through Abraham's family has not reached its final chapter.

The story is still unfolding.

And every generation must decide how it will step into it—whether it will repeat the old patterns of pride, fear, and self-protection, or whether it will choose the harder path of trust, humility, integrity, and forgiveness.

The Bible for Modern Life Series

This book is part of **The Bible for Modern Life** series—an ongoing collection that explores the meaning, historical setting, and message of individual books of Scripture.

Each volume looks closely at the biblical text to help readers understand what it meant in its original context and how its truths still apply to life today.

The goal is simple: to help modern readers engage more deeply with the Bible—one book at a time.

— Samuel Whitaker